Finance

Understanding Real Estate - Investing, Taxes and Wealth

Andy Anderson

Andy Anderson

Disclaimer Notice:

Please note the information contained within this document is for educational and entertainment purposes only. Every attempt has been made to provide accurate, up to date and reliable complete information. No warranties of any kind are expressed or implied. Readers acknowledge that the author is not engaging in the rendering of legal, financial, medical or professional advice.

Andy Anderson

Table of Contents

Introduction

I want to thank you for purchasing this book and hope you find the content useful and informative.

Even just a few centuries ago, the world economy was not as big or as booming as today is. The subsistence existence of human beings has shifted into what is accepted as a market economy in today's world, and the man with the most power is the man who can own, run and command a business that takes over a huge market share.

And in the competitive market scenario of today, real estate is becoming one of the most lucrative options, elevating the economic status of people from rags to riches. The average Joe turns into an overnight millionaire in this field – but beware! Like any business, risks exist here as well, and it is just as easy for a billionaire to become a pauper as it is for a normal man to end up a business tycoon. Making money is a matter of careful investments and taking calculated risks, instead of simply throwing around borrowed cash or family fortunes in a vain attempt to play the market.

A perk of the real estate industry is that one really does not need to possess a formal higher educational degree. Although there are fancy MBA degrees and the like which will give you a good look into the world of business and economics, one can handle themselves without too much difficulty even if one does possess any of those degrees. Education does not equal expertise, after all. What one really needs are good interpersonal and communication skills, along with a healthy dose of common sense and entrepreneurial spirit – mix it all together and you can definitely make a huge splash in the market!

Of course, as I mentioned, risks certainly exist. Dealing in property is no joke; it requires a delicate touch, especially considering how obscure the real estate market can turn out to be. Often times, people get into it, but unable to make it big, they end up giving up too soon. They make poor decisions, expecting too much in too short a time. What they do not realize is that the real estate market is a flexible market, allowing for some amazing investment options. Use these the right way, and you will be rolling in cash before you know it!

Of course, money is lost in huge chunks through the payment of taxes. Paying taxes is considered a cringe worthy activity, and for good reason. Having to part with hard earned money can seem like a tough task, but one that needs to be done to avoid trouble.

When it comes to paying taxes, people from the middle class are hit the worst, as the rich will find ways to evade taxes (and get away with it) and the poor are not taxed, given their low income.

Those stuck in between are made to pay hefty amounts of money and according to a survey conducted on the topic, several of the participants who took part- termed taxing as being a *"threat to their moral order and robbing hardworking citizens of their dignity"*.

It is understood that 65 to 75% of Americans hate to pay taxes, and their animosity against the government imposition runs deeper than appears. It runs in their veins; thanks to their ancestors, as a majority of the people had a problem paying taxes right from the times of kings and queens.

But what if I told you that it is possible to not pay a single dollar towards your property tax and get away with it? Wouldn't that be amazing? Well, the simple solution is to make timely investments! As I mentioned previously, the real estate business is lucrative, not only because of its nature itself, but also because it allows certain amount flexibility when it comes to investments! Although it might seem like a tough task to use real estate investments as a means to avoid taxes, it can be easy if done the right way. This way, you remain on the legal side of the law, play the market to your heart's content, become that classy business tycoon, and still manage to earn your millions safely!

Real estate investments are one of the safest and best options for you, to avoid paying taxes and build a large and wealthy empire. In this book, we will read on the right way in which you can invest in real estate and use it as a means to avail tax exemptions.

I will run you through the basics of buying and selling property and how you can break into a profit, by doing the same. The book will act as you one-stop real estate investment guide, and push you on the right path. I have divided it into two parts – the first part of the book is meant for the individual who wants invest in real estate he or she can follow these quick procedures to earn themselves a large amount of money by making use of tax laws and the like. I have expanded on what real estate is, how you can invest in it and the pros and cons of investing in different types of properties. Once you have gotten a clear picture of what real estate investment is, you can even go about beginning your own career as a real estate agent, building your own business.

That is what the second part of the book is. We will deal with the industry itself and how you can amass wealth by working in real estate. We will look at some strong strategies that you can employ to buy some brilliant properties and land the best deals. We will also identify the *'Don'ts'* of this industry and see how to exercise caution when making your deals so that you are not left with the short end of the stick.

Let us begin.

ć

Andy Anderson

Chapter 1

Understanding Real Estate, Investments And Taxes

Before we can get into the nitty gritty details of how you can make money in real estate – as an individual or as an entrepreneur – you will need to know what real estate investments are and how they are related to the taxes you pay. So in this chapter, I am going to quickly tell you what real estate is and how it is an investment and how taxes are connected to them.

In the simplest of terms, real estate can be defined as a property that comprises of land and the buildings constructed on top of it. The term is inclusive of all the natural resources that the land has, from the flora and the fauna to any minerals that may be mined from beneath the soil.

Now the general trend in the media and the public is to classify real estate as any property that is residential. You would have often seen real estate advertisements that show off beautiful, high-rise apartment condos or townhomes, with wonderful slogans and amazing pictures. While the residential homes *do* form a part of real estate, they are not the be all and end all of real estate investments. The reason they are generally taken to be the face of real estate investments is that these residential buildings are often more easily accessible than other types of real estate, which are commercial and recreational real estate.

As the name suggests, commercial real estate includes properties owned by commercial interests, like offices, warehouses, retail store buildings, etc. On the other hand, recreational real estate is filled with those properties that are meant to be used for recreational purposes, such as vacationing.

I have expanded more on the types of real estate in the following chapters, when we will take each one individually and look at the pros and cons of investing in them. Now, we will move on to understanding what an investment is.

To put it simply, an investment is a promise of a yield in the future in proportion to the amount of money you have invested. When you put in some cash, there will be a return for that capital amount in the future that is calculated on a yearly basis. Different types of investments will earn you different types of returns – bonds and cash savings in the banks yield interests, shares and debentures will give you dividends and so on and so forth. In real estate, the investment generally tends to be the amount of money you have put into buying a property and the returns vary, depending on whether you lease it out, rent it out or if you are reselling the property.

Real estate investments are extremely lucrative options, because they allow you to play with the tax laws and earn yourself some nice tax benefits to boost your wealth. I have expanded on this in the following chapters, but let me tell you what a tax benefit is.

Investopedia defines the term tax benefit as *"an allowable deduction on a tax return intended to reduce a taxpayer's burden while typically supporting certain types of commercial activity. A tax benefit allows some type of adjustment benefiting a taxpayer's tax liability."*

In simple terms, a tax benefit is when you can avoid paying certain taxes legally so that your wealth stays with you instead of going to the government. There are many different types of tax benefits that you can avail as an individual citizen, but in this book, we will concentrate on tax benefits from real estate investments and how you can avail them. Before we get into that, though, let me first tell you how real estate investments are taxed in America, so that you can get a basic understanding of the taxing system.

Ever since taxes were introduced in the late 1700's, people have looked for ways to avoid paying them. This is mainly because tax money is hardly used for the purpose that it is collected for, and more importantly, the tax rules vary from class to class.

The Internal Revenue Service collects taxes on behalf of the government and lays down the ground rules for taxation policies. These taxes are collected to fund their operations in part or in full.

Taxes can be categorized into four major components viz. Income tax, property tax, sales tax and other excise taxes. All of these are collectively known as federal taxes and can be levied on the same income, property or other activities, without offsetting each other.

Income tax is levied on a federal and state level and property taxes are mostly levied at the local level. But since most states have their own rules and regulations, the same property can be taxed at multiple levels.

Those are the different types of taxes you may be paying as an individual or a commercial establishment. Tax benefit in real estate can be more aptly termed as tax redemption, since you will have to play with the tax laws and work with the resources available to you in order to propound your wealth. We will discuss in detail how you can avail of these benefits available to you as a real estate investor in the later chapters.

It is extremely important that you understand how you will be taxed and remain prepared to fill up the forms and pay the loans on time.

Andy Anderson

Chapter 2
Quick Pointers To Keep In Mind When Investing In Real Estate

Now that you have an understanding of what real estate is and what taxes are, we can get into the more important details – investing! To begin with, you will need a basic knowledge of the things you need to consider while investing in real estate. You cannot just jump into buying random property simply because it looks good or has a low price. There are a number of factors you need to take into consideration when you choose invest so that your investment becomes a lucrative deal – otherwise you are going to end up at a loss. As you know, there are several factors to consider while buying property and you cannot settle for just about anything. You have to look for amenities and other such factors before zeroing in on the property.

Here is that list of things you will need to keep in mind when you begin investing in real estate.

Location of the property

Obviously, the most important things you need to consider are the location of the property. As per real estate, location is seen as the most important aspect and what everybody should look into first before making an investment. If the location is great, then that is half the job done for you. Sometimes, if a house you want to buy is being offered to you at a really low price, you may want to step back and make sure that it is located in an area that is suitable. Access to amenities like the local supermarket, the schools, the offices, etc – these are all things you will want to take into consideration. Many times, the location of the property will be extremely ideal but access to amenities will not be available. You must steer clear of such properties and try to find those that are situated in the ideal location.

Before you choose the site, try to have an idea of the ideal location for your project. If you work as per a set plan, you will easily find the best location for yourself. Look at the pictures that the owner has provided to you. You will be able to make your choice on whether to visit the site or not, based on these pictures. You will also not be caught by surprise; in case there are some flaws, and be prepared for all that the location of the site has on offer for you. You must also carry your camera along, and take pictures of the location. You can refer back to these pictures and easily plan your project.

It is a good idea to go there and inspect all the details by yourself. Spend at least a week in visiting the place you want to invest in and get a personal experience of what it feels like to live there by yourself. It is important that you look at the property in the morning and at night, as you need to see how much light filters in during the day. Look around the neighborhood and see what kind of people live there – will the environment suit you and your needs?   Will you be able to lease or rent out the property if you do not plan on living in it yourself and thereby make a good profit? Consider all these things before you buy the property.

Size of the property

The second thing to take into consideration when you purchase real estate is the size of the property. No matter what you are buying – a building, a house, and bare land – you cannot make a purchase without being aware of how much ground it covers. Ask the seller for proper details – you can even have it measured yourself to make sure that you are not cheated. Then, step back and ask yourself a couple of questions – is it big/small enough to be rented out at a particular amount? Will it suit the needs of a family or single people? Will you be able to make a sales pitch to prospective tenants without any problems?

Here too, it is best that you have a certain size in mind. Ensure that the size is slightly bigger than your expectations. Many people prefer to buy a large area and construct a small house on it. This will allow them lots of free space around the house or building. This space they will then utilize to expand their existing house or add another building. You can do the same with your location and ensure that there is enough free space to expand your current construction.

Carry a measuring instrument with you to measure the size of the property. It is ideal to have a set size in your mind and then visit the site. If the size is only a little off, then it is fine but if it is much smaller than what you were expecting then it is best that you move to the next.

Consider all factors keeping your budget and your purpose of purchase in mind before you buy the property.

Price of the property

The third factor you should be worried about is the price of the property. Obviously, you cannot afford to buy huge mansions when you start out, so make a budget that you can afford within your current income and then start looking for properties that match that limit. Many people make the mistake of not having a budget in mind and start hunting for property. Make sure you don't make the mistake and are prepared to buy a property that lies within your budget.

The budget depends on how much money you have at your disposal. It will differ from person to person. Try to have a limit that is easily repayable. If you are thinking of taking a loan, make sure the loan is small and that most of the money is yours and not borrowed. And even if you are borrowing, try to take it from family members.

You will have to choose the property you are buying based on your budget only. Now, you cannot allow yourself to be cheated on a sale, which means that you will have to do some research before you begin to invest! Look around the locality and check to see how much the true value of a property in that area is. Talk to the people living in the area – they are bound to know how much the rate per square foot, or per meter square, is. Once you have an idea of how much the property can be valued at loosely, you will know if you are being overcharged. If you are, find out why and start negotiating! It is always a good idea to start with a price that is much lower than what you are willing to spend on the property. Slowly make your way up but don't go all the way up. You must ideally stop at a price that is 5% lesser than what you wish to spend on the property. In fact, don't carry the entire amount with you. Take only a little and pay a certain advance to the owner. Then start bargaining and try to reduce the amount payable as much as possible.

Things included with the property

As I said before, you cannot allow yourself to be cheated out of hard earned money when you buy real estate. It is obvious that the land owner will not give you only a house or a piece of land. There will be some things that will come with it and you have to know what you will be getting or what you will need with the property. So, start by making a list of the basic necessities that you expect to get with your property. Having such a list handy will make it quite easy for you to find or go after what you want. Before you close the deal, check for all the things that the seller is offering to go along with the property itself. For instance, in residential purchases, the sellers tend to include fully furnished houses, which come with furniture and beautiful interiors. Recreational purchases, on the other hand, may come with fences, swimming pools or even livestock, while commercial establishments are often sold with the office furniture, the undergrounds storage units and the like. Look around for all that and make sure you have them al mentioned on the deed when you make the purchase.

Ask the owner in advance and have an idea of what is being given to you, along with your land. If in case you want something else then ask the owner to add it to the property. If he refuses to, then check how much it costs to have it installed. If it suits your budget then take the deal but if it is out of your budget, then it is best that you walk away from it. But if you really do like the property then you can talk it out with the owner and either get him to pay half or reduce the cost from your payment.

If none of these are present and the owner is still charging you a large sum, then it is best to walk away from the deal. You will find another place that offers you all of these amenities and at a good price. Even if you absolutely love the place, don't settle for it if it does not come with the standard amenities and fixtures and the owner is not obliging.

Also ensure that they are in the condition that the seller promised they would be in. you do not want to receive tattered furniture in what was supposed to be a fully furnished house. Make sure that everything is in order before *and* after you make the purchase.

Boundary of the property

Obviously, before you make the purchase, you will need to scout the property properly. When you are casing it out, make sure you are well aware of the boundary your property extends to. You need exactly where your ownership of the land ends and another's begins. Too often, people find that their lands encroach on another's and they did not even know when they bought it!

Knowing the boundary becomes especially important for recreational and commercial properties. For the latter, obviously, you cannot inconvenience another to run your business, and you may have to get high walls built to demarcate the end of your property. The same goes for the former; you may have to fence your boundary to show the end of your property so that your tenants do not end up trespassing on another's land.

Head out to the location yourself and take an engineer or site manager along if you have to. See to it that you understand all your boundaries properly and are operating within your limits. Don't assume things and make sure you know exactly where the boundaries of your properties lie and place the fence or wall. It does not have to be a big and heavy fence, just a few wooden dowels can be inserted and you can run some wire around it. The idea is to seal off the property such that people know it is your site and you are the absolute owner. You can also place a signboard on the same to ensure that people know whom the property belongs to.

Process of buying the property

So far, you have scouted the property and made note of things you will need to remember about the estate itself. Now comes the process of buying the house/land. As you know, it is not really a piece of cake to buy a property. It is more than going to the site and signing on the papers. It is important that the people does all the right things and not make mistakes.

More often than not, negotiations will take place between the buyer and the seller – they tend to be brutal, since both parties involved want the maximum out of the deal. The seller wants a big profit margin and as the buyer, you do not want to pay anything more than the minimum price. Be calm and be assertive; don't try to cheat your seller out of a couple grand, but do not be taken in yourself either. When you have managed to arrive at a consensus, draw up the deed.

It can be a good idea at this stage to get your lawyer involved. Make sure he goes through all the details and peruses the deal inside out so that you are not left wanting. Wait until your lawyer can approve of it; when he does, go ahead and make the payment that will allow you to become the absolute owner of the property! Following this will be the important paper work you will have to file – get your lawyer to guide you through it and before you know it, you have made your first real estate investment! The process of buying a house can differ slightly if you are looking to invest in a foreign country. We will look at it in great detail in the last few chapters of this book.

Let us look at the different steps that you must adopt when you wish to buy an ideal property.

Financing your purchase

You have negotiated the price and your lawyer has given you the okay to go ahead – now you need arrange for the finance to make the payment. Not everybody has pockets deep enough to invest in real estate out of their own savings or income. You will need to look around you and scope of potential moneylenders, from commercial banks to creditors, who can help you out with the purchase.

The best option is, of course, a commercial bank; it is also safe and formal, which means that everything is transparent for you to work with. Choose a bank that gives you the ideal price and interest. It pays to personally know someone at the bank, as they will guide you through the best prices. Collect all the documents necessary, from your personal documents to the property's documents, and then file them with the institution. It may take some time for the loan to get approved, but once it does come through, you can make the payment – you're a proud owner of a new house! Keep in mind though, that banks often give only 80% of the amount you are going to pay for the property – the remaining 20% you will have to arrange for by yourself. It is also a good idea to approach a credit union. These are places where you can avail a quick loan at a discounted price. But you need to be a member at such a union if you want the loan or personally know someone who is a member. You can also try borrowing from your peers. They might be willing to lend you a small amount at a good rate of interest. Dip into your savings, ask your relatives for a quick loan or approach other moneylenders, but make sure you get everything in order before you make the purchase!

Future prospects of the property

Keep in mind what the future of the property you are buying is going to be. Real estate investments are often about buying and reselling houses; while you may live in it as soon as you buy the house, remember that you could also sell it at a later date. For that reason, make sure that the house you are buying has the potential to increase in value rather than depreciate wholly.

Ask around and see how the prices have been varying in the past. If the trend is a good one then stick with it. Try to assess how much the property will be valued at in the future.

Check the area you are buying into to see if the value of the property there *will* increase. Also check to see what other type of properties are there, what might be built there in the future, what commercial establishments exist, etc. A good idea is to invest in a locale that is still growing; the prices will be low enough that you can definitely afford it and the value of your property will only appreciate as the growth potential of the area begins to be fulfilled.

Satisfaction and purpose of purchase

Buying a house does not just mean purchasing the most lucrative option that is. Most people, when they invest in real estate initially, mean to live in the house they buy. If you are one such person, then make sure that the property you want to purchase is to your liking and suits your needs. Do not just blindly go with other's suggestions – make your own assessments, based on the locality, the size, the pricing, etc.

Do several inspections of the property you wish to buy, and get to know everything about it so that you are not cheated. Also keep in mind the reason you are buying the property – if you are not going to live there, are you going to rent or lease it out? If so, then approach the purchase from that perspective; what will a prospective tenant be interested in? How much will they be willing to pay as rent and how much should you charge based on the general price trend of the area?

Take into account all external and internal factors about the property before you decide to spend your money on it. Make sure it is going to give you a return in the future – whether through a resale or a tenant, it does not matter, as long as the property gives you a return value. Otherwise, it becomes a dead weight and not a real investment, which defeats the purpose of real estate in the first place.

Andy Anderson

Chapter 3

Residential Real Estate Properties

As I mentioned previously, there are three major types of real estate properties you can invest in. I told you about the factors to keep in mind when spending your money – here are the pros and the cons of investing in each type of real estate. To begin with, we will go with the most popular type of real estate – residential real estate, like apartment buildings and condos that you can live in or lease out to a tenant.

What is Residential Real Estate?

As the name suggests, residential properties are those that are used for residential purposes – where people can live, either as a family or as a single person. That means the kinds of buildings you can classify under this category of real estate are –

- Independent houses

- Villas

- Apartments

- Condominiums

- Hostels

Remember, these are places where people live – no business venture can take place here unless the owner agrees to such a clause. Owners also tend to make a specific mention of the exact number of people that can live in the property; especially maintenance costs will go up when there are more people sharing the same space. If the house is meant only for a family of 4 members, then he will mention it in the rent deed – if the tenant brings in more people than arranged for, then he is liable to the owner, maybe even for legal action.

But there can be some who will own the entire building and not care how many are living in the house. In fact, the more the people, the better the rent. But the person has to abide by the local country's rules.

There are single-family properties and multifamily properties you can invest in. The former – as is obvious from the name – refers to individual houses you can rent out to one family. The latter refers to properties contain several houses, like a township, where different families take one house each. It could even be an apartment building with different homes for different families.

A single house can be used in any way that you like. It entirely depends on how much money you are trying to make out of your investment. Although the main goal for any investor is to make the most of the investment, it pays to choose a type wisely.

When you invest in a residential property, either you can choose to live in it or rent it or least it out to tenants. To do that, you need to know how to charge them. Rent for residential properties can be charged on the basis of –

• *Only rent* – here, the tenant pays only a fixed amount that you have asked for in the rent deed. As the owner, you will have to pay for the maintenance of the building by yourself.

• *Rent and maintenance costs* – in the rent deed, both you and your tenant agree that it will be the tenant who will pay for the upkeep of the building; along with the monthly rent sum he or she owes you.

• *Lease payments* – under this type of renting out the house, you – as the owner – collect a lump sum of money from the tenant at the beginning when they move in and then rent it out for the next few years.

Now when you rent out residential property, there are certain things expected of the house you are going to be giving your tenants. Standard fittings and fixtures are the norm and you will have to provide for them before you rent it out, unless your tenant specifically denies wanting them, which is a rare case indeed. Here are those fixtures you will have to make sure your residential property has –

- Ceiling and/or wall-mounted fans

- Tube lights

- Switch ports

- Well maintained toilets with proper plumbing

- Cupboards

- Parking space

Making sure you have all these amenities provided for will definitely help you increase your rent price. Other things like furniture and chimneys are also options you can offer your tenants for an increased price. All these are value additions that will draw prospective tenants to your residential property like moths to a flame. But it is best to have a flexible option. If the tenant does not want these then you should immediately have the option of removing it immediately.

As you know, not everything will be perfect and you must consider the pros and cons of any property before investing in it. Here are the advantages and disadvantages to investing in a residential property and the renting it out to a tenant.

Pros

• Unless you are looking to buy and rent a huge, palatial place like a mansion, your initial investment is not going to be very big. Residential properties are very affordable, since most people buy houses to live in them themselves, which means that you need not have a huge sum of money to begin your investment. A few thousand dollars will be enough – you do not need millions. You will also not have to borrow a hefty loan for it and can manage within a little money.

• An extension of the previous idea, since you do not need millions of dollars to buy your property, you can easily arrange for the finance you will need to make the purchase. Banks approve loans for housing very quickly; within weeks, you will have the money you need to make the purchase. Submit a few documents, attend a few calls from the bank and up to 80% of the total amount you have to pay for will be at available to you within the space of a month, following which you can rent out without any difficulty. These days, many banks offer a 90% loan amount. So you only have to invest 10% in it. The time period to repay these will also be quite big and you can easily repay it within a short period of time.

• This type of investment is ideal for youngsters, as they can own a property with whatever money they have at their disposal. They don't have to move into the property and just renting it out will help them make back some of the money that they have spent on buying the property. It is also possible for the youngster to lease the property and make back the money slowly through interest derived from the lease amount. Doing so will motivate the youngster to keep going and make bigger and better real estate investments in the future.

• Loan and mortgage money are applicable for tax deductions; house renovations costs are also tax deductibles, which means that you stand to save a lot of money.

• Compared to commercial properties, residential properties are cheaper while still being bigger in terms of square foot. The cost per square foot is far lesser, which means you get a larger piece of land for a lesser amount of money.

• Owning an apartment building means you yourself can live in one of the apartments, while renting the rest out to tenants. You can keep an eye in them, and also have you plugged into the maintenance of the building, which you can manage without too much hassle. You also get to know about any damages or any problems immediately.

Cons

• The biggest problem in investing in residential property is that you are entirely dependant on your tenants for your returns. This means that if you do not have a tenant to rent your apartment out to, then you do not earn any returns on the investment you made while buying the property. This is one reason why single-family properties are so risky – until such a time when you can find someone to rent the house, it will remain empty and you will still have to pay maintenance costs in order to keep it in good condition. So it is safer to buy an apartment building or any multifamily property that will make sure you have a consistent amount of rent coming to you regularly. It may be a bit more expensive, but it is certainly a safer option.

• It is obvious that you will be uncomfortable renting out your condo. You would have paid a large sum for it and the house will be extremely valuable to you. If you end up giving it to the wrong person then you will have to deal with several issues. It will also be a pain getting them to vacate. You will have to put in a lot of effort to do so.

• Unless specifically mentioned in the rent deed, maintenance of the building is usually taken care of by the owner, though the tenant may share the cost. If there is a leak or a pipe break, then the tenant will expect the owner – that is, you – to have it fixed and that too as soon as possible, without the slightest delay. Costs of repair can be high and you may need to set aside specific budgets for repairs from your overall income if you want to be effective.

• Obviously, residential properties are meant to be given out to families for living in the houses. Sometimes, you may want to offer it to commercial establishments who offer to pay much more than an individually tenant ever could. This is not illegal, but it is a definite hassle – you must make sure that you have all the permission from all the necessary authorities to ensure that a business can be run out of that residential property. If you do not get this permission, you may be in trouble, even be in danger of losing your property. You must also check with the other residents in the area to make sure that they are not troubled with the idea of a commercial establishment operating within their midst.

• If it is a hostel that you are renting out – say goodbye to your peaceful times! Generally, the only people who come to live in hostels and dorms are youngsters who need accommodation while they work or study in universities. They are not too bothered about maintenance or upkeep of the building, and may even have difficulty paying you rent regularly. It is very possible that you will receive your rent from different people each month! And youngsters are always looking to break rules, so be prepared for others being snuck in, late night parties and midnight snacks interrupting your schedules! Don't think you can easily control them as one spat and they will be gone the next day. It is never a good idea to rent out to hostels, as the tenants will not be to your liking at all.

• You might not be able to afford a house if your credit score is bad. That might set you back mentally and you will think that it is impossible for you to invest in real estate. So it is best that you have your credit checked at the earliest. If it is bad, then have it rectified to improve your chances of availing a loan.

• You will have to constantly keep an eye on what your tenant is up to. There is the danger of your tenant subletting your apartment to someone else at a higher rate than what he or she is paying you, leaving you running at a loss. It could also be that the tenant is up to shady activity within your premises, which means that the police could close down your building and leave you with no income. You will always have to keep checking in with your tenant and make sure everything is above board and that you are not getting cheated at any point of time. If you do not get along well with your tenants, this may be difficult to do and you may want to think about replacing them with someone else.

• This type is probably not suitable for foreign investments as you will have invested quite a bit in the property and it might get a bit difficult for you to make the money back. You might have to wait a long time before making the money back, especially if your property is an area that is not suitable for occupancy. So you might have to reconsider your investment.

Keep all these pros and cons of investing in different residential properties in mind before you choose to go in for them. Despite the few difficulties you may face in renting or leasing out your property, residential real estate is a brilliant way to make a steady income, since the tenants are required to pay you on a monthly basis. It is a definite return that is also steady, which means that there is a constant flow of cash into your account. Take into account all factors and then make the investment – you will not regret it!

Chapter 4
Commercial Real Estate Properties

Residential properties are a safe investment, allowing you a definite return and a reward for the initial money you put in. Commercial properties, on the other hand, are a little bit trickier and require a careful hand to navigate them, though they are just as lucrative and give good returns too!

In this chapter, we will look at commercial real estate properties in detail. Right from its meaning to its pros and cons, we will look at what it means to own a commercial property and why you should be investing in one.

What is Commercial Real Estate?

As the name suggests, commercial real estate property is any property that is used solely for business purposes. So these are buildings that are used as hotels, shopping malls, office buildings and so on and so forth. Obviously, investing in such buildings and then leasing them out to commercial establishments brings in far more money that residential properties, but the initial payment you have to make is also pretty big.

Now what you must keep in mind while buying such property is that the buildings must be enormous – they must be able to hold large numbers of people at once, from workers and employees to customers and clients of the establishment that is renting it. Obviously, when you choose to rent your building out to commercial establishments, they are going to be looking for such qualities, which means that you will have to take it into consideration when you buy the property.

Another factor you must consider is the area; the locale where you are buying the property must be conducive to business and that too, a particular type of business that you wish to rent to. For instance, if it is a shopping mall that you want to rent out to, then you will have to ensure that the building you buy is huge, placed within the city so that all prospective buyers have access to the shops and scout for sellers who are willing to place their stores within your building.

Many people forgo checking whether there really is a demand for a certain type of building in a particular area. This is mostly for those that wish to construct a building. If you don't check if your building will have enough takers then you will stand to lose from your investment. So make sure you check out how many people are actually interested in the property and whether it will be easy for you to rent it out to commercial establishments.

Generally, the commercial properties are leased out on a contract basis for a number of years, at the end of which the ownership of the building reverts back to you. This is to save time and effort, since collecting large sums of money as rent each month can be cumbersome. Commercial property can be leased out on the basis of the following –

•   *A gross lease*, where the tenant pays only the rent on the property. As the owner, you must take over the payment of the property tax, the insurance as well as the maintenance money for the whole building.

•   *A single net lease*, where the tenant pays both the rent due to you as well as the property taxes for the space he is assuming, though the maintenance and the insurance still fall under your purview.

•   *A double net lease*, where the tenant pays rent to you, takes care of the property tax as well as the insurance. As the owner you will only have to worry about the maintenance costs.

• *The triple net lease*, which is the most lucrative deal for you, wherein the tenant pays everything, from the rent owed to you to the maintenance and upkeep of the building. As owner, you have little to no worries and you only need to keep an eye on the property until the lease ends.

Like with the residential properties, the commercial properties are also expected to have certain basic add-on features to go with the building itself. These are the amenities required to run a proper business establishment, and offering them to your tenants will definitely increase both your rent price as well as your credibility as a landlord. Here are a few of those things you will need to make sure your building has before you lease it out to any commercial establishment –

• Proper parking space that is spacious enough to accommodate a certain number of cars

• Proper electricity to all parts of the building with enough lighting

• Good internet coverage with a strong Wi-Fi connection that spreads to all parts of the building

• Proper space for a canteen or a cafeteria, preferably furnished with long tables and chairs

- A good water source so that the people in the building have a drinking water

- Little cubicles or work stations for individual employees, preferably furnished with tables and chairs

Of course, what the interiors of the office space looks like will depend on the particulars of the business you want to rent your building out to. For instance, if it is a shopping mall that you are investing in, then having little cubicles or workstations does not make sense, since most of the rooms will end up being retail outlets for different brands.

It may be a good idea to allow your tenant to customize the building after you rent it out. Make sure to have it all drawn up in legal contracts, though, so that you are not cheated. What you need to do is to have the purpose of the commercial establishment you are leasing out to in mind when you start furnishing the place so that you can find tenants easily without too much hassle.

Like with the residential properties, commercial real estate also comes with its own pros and cons. These can be classified as follows –

Pros

•   The biggest advantage of a commercial space to rent out is that maintenance costs tend to come down. It may seem like a bit of a stretch, but believe me, your tenants themselves will look after the space as best as they can! This is because they are most likely to be retailers and sellers of some product themselves, which means that their offices will be frequented by prospective buyers and clientele. This automatically translates to keeping their office space clean and tidy so that they make a good impression. As an owner, you will not have to worry about the upkeep of the building, though you may have to pay some amount towards maintenance, depending on the type of lease agreement you have with your tenants.

•   Your value as a real estate investor will increase several folds, if you own a commercial property. This is mainly because people will look at you as a bona fide investor, who is capable of making the right investment choices. Other people will be willing to invest in your ventures and you will find it extremely easy to attract partners for your real estate investments.

•   Issues are easily resolved, since the relationship you will have with these tenants is entirely professional. Both you and the tenant are business owners; you run your own real estate and he runs his own business and together, you want to make money in your respective fields. The mutual symbiosis ensures that problems are solved in an easy manner, unlike with residential tenants who can make things personal and cause difficulty.

• As long as you are not planning to buy an entirely new building and then convert it into a commercial property, leasing policies are easy to handle. All you are doing is buying the property from the previous owners who already have tenants – the building simply changes hands and comes to you. In this case, you simply need to model your own leasing agreements based on the previous owner's pricing policy; you have little research work to do on how much you should charge your tenants. If you are creating a new commercial property, though, then you will have a bit of work to do, from renovation to research on the pricing trends to make sure you get the right amount of money due to you.

• Renting out for commercial purposes means you stand to make a lot of money in very little time. Obviously, businesses pay much more than an individual, which means that you rake in a lot of cash. A good idea would be to lease it out for a long period of time. That way, you can earn a lump sum, which you could use to pay off the loans you got from the bank to make your investments in the first place. Whatever is left over, you can reinvest in other fields, maybe even another real estate property, to double the value of the money. The best would be to go in for a triple lease system, since that is the most lucrative option – you don't have to worry about any costs and only need to keep an eye on your space.

• Barring sudden emergencies, you can expect that your tenants will not disturb you during the nights. Unless you specifically rent out to establishments that work night times as well, you can be sure that the tenants will go home in the evening. You can kick back after office hours are over and not worry about any problems to fix in the dead of the night.

• This type of investment might be ideal for foreign country investments mainly because of the low level maintenance that is involved. You won't have to spend a lot of time and energy looking into the matters and the company that is leasing it out will take care of the building. So, not only will you have a foreign property but also one that is hassle free and easy to take care of.

Cons

• The biggest disadvantage to investing in commercial properties is the huge amount if initial investment you will have to shell out at the beginning. Since it is not just one small home you are buying, you will have to have an enormous amount of startup capital – perhaps even a couple of millions – to begin your venture. Added to this will be the cost of repairing and sprucing up the place before you lease it out, all of which adds up to a hefty sum of money that is not easy to arrange for. The upside of this point is that the return you receive will be equally high; the businesses you rent out to will pay you in millions as well, which means that you can earn it back relatively quickly.

• Now obviously, when you rent out to commercial establishments, you are going to be dealing more than one tenant at any given time. Your building will probably host a number of businesses, perhaps one on each floor and that means you will have to deal with a lot of different people. As the owner, you will be stuck playing mediator if they do not get along well with one another. You are essentially the building's manager, and that job can be a nightmare. You will have to get them to agree with each other and see eye to eye, which may not always be easy. You are going to need excellent interpersonal skills and a bucket load of patience to deal with such problems!

• Another problem will arise if you are sharing the investment with someone else. The two of you might not be able to decide on who resolves the issues that arise out of the building.

• A youngster can forget about owning such a property. It will require a lot of money, which the youngster might not have at his disposal. In fact, it might not be possible for a lot of people to buy such types of properties, as it will require a lot of money that will have to be pooled in and invested to buy such a property.

• Unless you have specifically gone in for the triple lease, you are still responsible for the upkeep of your building. Since commercial properties will inevitably be open to the general public, they are also prone to more damage than residential properties. People will go in and go out regularly, and some may end up causing damage to your property. Rash driving could harm the parking lot; the dustbins could be treated carelessly, so on and so forth. While the individual establishments may have been contracted to pay maintenance for the upkeep of their own spaces, the common spaces like parking lots or elevators will definitely fall under the purview of the owner – you. It may be a bit of a headache to keep these things in order, so you may have to hire a third party to do the upkeep and the maintenance of the whole building.

Despite the many different cons of the commercial properties, they are quite the lucrative deal if you are able to handle them well. They rake in millions of dollars and allow you to earn back your initial investment much earlier than a residential property would. There are difficulties and you will have to cater to the specific needs of the different businesses that will occupy your office spaces, but in the end, it is far more profitable than a residential property, which can give you only a couple of thousand dollars a month at the most.

Once again, keep in mind your budget and the purpose of your purchase before you choose to invest in commercial real estate!

Andy Anderson

Chapter 5

Recreation Real Estate Properties

In the last two chapters, we looked at commercial properties and residential properties and now, we will look at the third type known as recreational properties. In this chapter I will give you information on the meaning of these types of properties and pros and cons of investing in them.

What is Recreational Real Estate?

The word recreation is associated with pleasure and joy and for good reason. Recreational properties are meant for the sake of rest and relaxation to whomever you rent it out to. Most such properties tend to be farms, ranches, waterfronts, zoos, wild life reserves, etc. People prefer picturesque locations to retire to when vacationing and relaxing, and more often than not, nature ends up being the perfect background for them to get away from the madness and the hustle and bustle of the real world.

I'm sure you have watched television shows that showcase certain unique houses that people have built for their recreation. These are recreational houses that are meant to provide the owner with recreational pleasure. There are some unique creations all over the world and they are meant to serve as people's second homes. But you can also choose to make it your primary home.

When you are renting out property as recreational estate, you will have to decide if you want to open it to the general public or keep it for private tenants. For instance, if you buy a small cabin close to the forest, or a sea front shack, you could probably lease it out to families for vacation on a seasonal basis. But if you own a large piece of land you want to turn into a recreational property open to the public, you could consider furbishing it as a zoo or a wild life reserve or something similar.

Now, when you are dealing with large plots of land that you want to lease out or rent out, you will have to follow a couple of rules set up by the authorities first. You will need to get your land 'zoned' – zoning is the process by which the concerned authorities of the government decide how the land can be used. You may not always be able to buy such a huge piece of land as required by the property you want to lease out; generally, the local municipal authorities zone such large tracts of land seasonally. You will have to go through a number of legal procedures to get permission to begin using the land. Consult a lawyer and have them help you through the procedures so that you can make the most out of it!

Once you have control of the land and you can start constructing a zoo or a reserve or a cabin – whatever your specifics are – you will have to make provisions for those usual expected features that come of any real estate. Just like with the residential and the commercial properties, here too you will have to have standard fixtures, some of which are –

•   Fences and gates to demarcate the boundaries of your land; this becomes especially important in the cases of large, public properties like zoos or reserves, since there are animals to be looked after as well as a rowdy public that will need to be controlled

•   Sheds and cabins with electricity and water supply; if you are offering a retreat in the woods or a place to camp out, these are going to be in high demand, since your tenants will need to stay comfortable

•   Waste disposal systems, since you cannot afford to let the place become a dump.

•   Transport facilities that will help people travel in and out of the countryside. It is important that you make arrangements for people to move around especially if the retreat is located far from shops and other amenities. If you don't offer them such facilities then it might get a bit inconvenient for them. You have to try and maintain cabs with drivers that will drive people around.

•   You can also have a few basic necessities so that your guests can buy them in case of emergencies.

Unlike with residential or commercial properties, there is no hard and fast rule for the fixtures that will be in demand. It will have to be customized according to the purpose of the property. For instance, if it is a zoo that you are opening, it is expected that there are fences around the individual cages to protect both the animals and the public. Having electricity here may be a waste of money. On the other hand, if you are renting out a cabin in the woods, the tenants will definitely need at least the barest minimum of amenities like a couple of lights to see by, even if they are looking for a rustic experience. Take all these into account when you decide to invest in recreational real estate.

Pros

•   Considering that most recreational properties remain close to nature in some way or another, you are assured of having tenants. Public properties like zoos and reserves will have year-round visitors, but the cabins and retirement homes may be more seasonal in nature. Despite that, you will rake in a lot of money, especially during the summers. More and more people are flocking towards nature and are looking for seasonal cabins to rent and enjoy a truly natural experience, which means that you will not be left with a want of tenants to rent out to. It pays to do some research and look at areas that are popular for their tourist attractions. It is ideal to choose locations that are popular all through the year and not only for certain months.

•   Here too, you will find it easy to have other people invest with you. They will like your choice of investment and decide to join hands with you, in order to have a lucrative deal. You can tie up with someone interested in recreational property investments and expand your existing property with their help. Ultimately, you will stand to gain a great deal out of your recreational property investment, provided you choose the right kind.

•   If you offer a couple of add on amenities and services like hiking, rafting, fishing, etc, you will be sure to draw a huge number of people wanting to participate in such adventure sports. You could even enter into a partnership with some of the locals to manage your property for you; they could turn it into a proper, thriving business venture that offers more than just housing for the clients. Here too, it is best to choose the best location and the best people to team up with. One way or another, you will easily find someone or the other wanting to rent out your place.

• Animal lovers and conservationists are among the many tenants who will flock to your property. Unlike the general public who come, stay for a while, relax and then leave, these people have their jobs centered on some of the services you may offer. That means that you have tenants to hire out to even in the off-season, and you could even avail their expertise in the area of nature to spruce up all that you offer! For instance, if you are renting you cabin out to a marine biologist, you could ask him or her to host a couple of exhibits for the tourists for a small fee!

• A good idea is to buy a place that is just in early developmental stage. Prices of such spots will be cheaper, and you will be able to spend more money on renovating it and setting up the way you like. As the area behind to develop, you will definitely be able to make a good profit out of your property!

Cons

• When you do have tenants, you will be making quite a bit of money. However, most recreational property tends to be seasonal, which means that off-season will leave you unsatisfied with only a meager amount of money coming in as compared to tourist seasons. Also, you must keep in mind the target audience – not all of them are used to the wilderness. Most of them will be from the city and so, escaping to a cabin in the woods will not seem like a fun vacation, especially to the kids of today. You will have to package your deal beautifully and offer add-on services to entice them into renting from you.

• Maintenance of the property can be very difficult. Living in the wilderness means that there will a number of daily chores to be performed to keep the property in good, living conditions. These chores can range from chopping wood for fire to shoveling the snow, and unless you can afford to spend all day doing such things all through the time that there are no tenants, you may have to hire the locals to help out. It can get quite labor intensive and costly.

• Again, tenants may complain that there are not enough drainage systems, water facilities and heating systems, etc. The truly city bred kids will also walk in expecting facilities like internet and Wi-Fi and telephone signals, which they may or may not receive in such remote places. You will have to be extra patient in dealing with such grumpy tenants, and arrange for whatever they require urgently.

• Considering the fact that you are building property close to nature and the wilderness, there is a very good chance that you will be exposed to extreme weather conditions. Be ready for thunder and snowstorms, landslides and heat waves and any such natural disaster. Have contingency plans ready in case of an emergency and make sure you have at least one of two medical facilities easily available to your tenants so that they are not caught unawares.

• You will have to be well aware of the danger that animals pose to your property and your tenants. Those properties that are situated closer to the woods in particular will have to be carefully cordoned off to prevent wild animals from creeping in; you still will not be able to do much about the rats and raccoons and the little animals that will creep in anyway. Provide your tenants with the right kind of protection so that they remain safe while enjoying the wilderness to the fullest. If there are incidents of people being attacked by animals then it is important that you take action and prevent any such incidents from occurring in the future.

• As we said before, recreational lands are subject to the whims and fancies of many concerned authorities. Expansion or renovation will be highly challenging for you. With residential or even commercial properties, you can expand as you wish to and the legal procedures will not take more than a couple of days or weeks to go through. On recreational lands, though, you may end up waiting months for the permits to fall through, and you will have to keep the authorities posted of your every move, since the safety of people could be at stake otherwise.

• Finding locals to keep in your employ could be quite tough. A lot of times, these recreational lands have communities that are closely knit and find it difficult to trust outsiders. Still if you could spin that around to your advantage and offer them generous employment, you will win their loyalty, which will go a long way in making sure your property is safe, clean and secure.

As you can see, of the three types of real estate to invest in, recreational real estate is the one that takes the most work. As a beginner to investing in real estate, you may want to stay away from it – it requires a lot of money, time and effort that you may or may not have at your disposal. On the other hand, if you have been in business for a while and you know the ins and outs and you have the resources to spare, recreational real estate could prove to be a strong investment that brings in a lot of money for you! Involve the locals and turn it into a proper tourist attraction and you will find that you are able to earn quite a lump sum, as compared to residential or even commercial properties!

Container homes

Container homes are new types of investments. They are modern day investments and are not like any of your previous types of investments. In this chapter, we will look at container homes in detail and look at their different aspects in detail.

Meaning

As the name suggests, "container homes" are made out of "containers". Now you will wonder as to what these containers are. Well, these are containers that are used in the shipping industry. They are cargo containers that are used to transport cargo from one country to another.

These containers are large in size and can hold several thousands of kgs of cargo. They are quite sturdy and capable of resisting wear and tear.

These containers make for great storage options and are used as go-downs by many small, and large, businesses.

Those looking for a quick house to set up also use them as housing choices. They are extremely sturdy and you can actually build entire houses using them. They are easily available and you can buy them from a container company.

Being unconventional, these types of houses are now slowly gaining popularity. You don't need a big investment for them and can manage within a fixed budget. Once you make use of these, you will be surprised at how beautiful they really can be. You can always choose them as a secondary choice and not a permanent one. You will have the satisfaction of having a secondary home, which you can rent out or live at yourself.

How to

When it comes to container homes, there are certain standard steps that you need to adopt. Let us look at these steps in detail:

The very first step is to look for the best location where you can set up your container home. Container homes can be set up at any location provided it is easy to transport the container. Look for a location that is to your looking. Most people prefer lands that are fully covered in grass as they make for good container home sites. You can look for good deals on sites. It is also a great idea to look for a recreational land where there is a natural attraction like waterfalls or mountains. This will add to your location's value and your house will be much more valuable.

The next step is to plan your container home. Look up some designs and choose a container size that will fit your land the best. You can choose to have a single container or layer up by placing one next to the other. You can create a duplex if you like.

The next step is to look for a container dealer who can supply the container to you. Most container suppliers will be located near the coast and you must look for the best one. Look at their online site and see if you like their designs. Some companies provide you with custom designs to suit your needs. You can provide them with a design idea and get them to create a custom container for you.

The next step is to head down and buy the container. You might have to travel quite a bit if you live away from the coast. You must also take an appropriate vehicle that can help you transport the container back to your land.

Once you buy the container/ containers, you must transport them to your site. The next step is to place them in the appropriate place. As was mentioned before, you must plan your house structure in advance and place the containers in the appropriate places. You can choose to make a duplex out of it.

Once everything is in place, you can decorate them, as you like. You can have them painted on the inside out and decorate everything in a way that you like.

Next, you can either rent it out or move in yourself.

Pros

• There are many pros of investing in container homes. The first pro is that, you can easily set up a container home. You need not come up with an elaborate plan and it will not take you more than a week to decide on a container home for yourself. You also do not have to wait a long time to have your home ready. All it will take is looking for the right place to set up your home and the right container that will turn into your home.

• The next advantage is the low costs. Apart from the land cost, the containers will not cost you much. So you can easily save on a lot of money by investing in a container home.

• The low cost makes it ideal to be your second home. You can expand your real estate investments by choosing to invest in container homes.

• The unique structure of these houses helps you be as creative as possible. You can decorate it in any which way that you like.

• You can easily transport your container homes as well. You can empty the contents of the container and attach it to a tow truck that can help you change the location of the home and transport it to a picturesque area. It will be like having a transportable home.

Cons

• The main con of this type of investment is that, it is tough to transport the container from one place to another. It will be extremely difficult for you to transport the containers and there is also the risk of damage that you must bear in mind.

• Since containers are made of metal, the risk of rust is quite prominent. Your container home might develop rust and you will have to spend on removing the rust from the container. It might be a bit more risky to stack the containers on top of each other as they might burden the bottom container.

• It is also quite difficult to adjust to a container home. It will be radically different from living in a regular house and you will have to do with several adjustments. It is also quite tough to fit in furniture into your container homes.

These form the different pros and cons of container homes. Overall, they are a great investment choice for you.

Andy Anderson

Chapter 6

Real Estate And Tax Redemption

So far we have talked about the different types of real estate that exist and what the benefits and disadvantages to investing in each of them are. From investment, we move on to tax, which I have already given you an introduction to earlier. Taxes can be levied on individuals, businesses, states, trusts and other organizations. In this book, we will only concentrate on the taxes that are levied on property and how you can avoid paying them. Remember, these are strategies that are mostly geared toward the individual real estate investor, though as a real estate agent you should be aware of them! As a single, layman, here are the things you can do to avoid paying too much tax.

Buy a house

When you buy a new house, you will be allowed to deduct two of the biggest expenses from your federal income tax viz. your property tax and the interest on your mortgage. These two are the biggest long-term deductions and there can be other small one-time deductions such as the points you pay at closing. When you fill out your tax returns, you must itemize your deductions. Once you become a homeowner, you will be able to deduct hefty amounts from your gross income. When you make the purchase, and before you fill out your returns form, you must enquire about all the deductions that you are entitled to before you pay out the year's taxes. Along with the mortgage interest and points, you will get to deduct some of the expenses that you incurred during the settlement. You must try and deduct as much as you can and bring it down to the bare minimum. If you do not deduct everything that there is to, in the year of your purchase, then you can amortize it and deduct it over the course of your loan period.

Renting it

If you decide to rent out your property, you will invite a tax on the rent that you receive. Say for example: if you rent it out for 1000$ a month, then you must declare this amount to the IRS, when you file your returns. But it is possible to reduce the tax by a large margin. In order to minimize the tax that you pay on your rental amount, you must produce bills such as safety insurance costs, mortgage interests, estate agent's fees, legal accountancy fees, repair costs, safety checks and council tax.

This will allow you to make a profit on your rent and further the benefit provided to you by your property.

Renovating your property

If you buy a house that needs a lot of renovation, then you will have access to a bonus, in terms of tax benefits. When you do up your house, you are sure to incur some costs, which you can deduct from your income tax. But remember that you must renovate the basic structure of the house in order to make it livable and not improve an existing feature. Costs incurred to improve the house will not qualify and won't be deducted from your income. So painting, fixing broken faucets etc. will not qualify as your renovations. They need to be solid renovations such as constructing an entirely different room from scratch, adding a false ceiling to protect from cold or heat etc.

As is apparent, investing in real estate will only work to your advantage and you will be able to save quite a bit on your taxes

.

Andy Anderson

Chapter 7

How To Buy and Sell In Loop

In the previous chapter, we looked at how you can buy a house, rent it and avoid paying taxes and now, we will understand how you can sell your current house and buy another one, to break into a profit.

We have already looked at how it is possible to avoid paying taxes for your real property. And now, we will read about buying and selling property, which can help you earn thousands of dollars.

Here are the steps that you need to follow and the criteria that will help you do the same.

Sell your house

The very first thing that you must do is sell your house. You must look for a great deal and sell it for a large profit. The tax law will exempt you from paying any taxes after you sell your property, provided that you have stayed there for a minimum of two years out of the last five or have owned it for the last 2 years. While there, you can do up the house in any which that way you like and try and make it as attractive as possible, in order to sell it for a good price.

Here is an extract of the law from the IRS website:

If you have a gain from the sale of your main home, you may qualify to exclude up to $250,000 of that gain from your income.

Buy a new one

The next step is to buy a new house. As was explained earlier, this will allow you to avoid paying your taxes. You will be eligible for all the same deductions and this will allow you to pay zero taxes. When you buy a new house, you must always buy it at a value that is below par. For this, you will have to scour for the best deal and be in constant touch with your agents. If you are doing it on your own, then you must be on the lookout for a good deal. You can look for a house that needs quite a bit of fixing, as that will allow you a tax benefit. If the house is not in a livable condition, then you can rent another one until such time as it is ready to be occupied. If you avail a loan for your house and it includes money required to do it up, then you can deduct the interest on the amount from your income.

Timing

It is important to buy your house early in the year and not during the months of September through December, as you will be behind on your taxes. Many rookies make the mistake of buying their houses in September or October, but this is a wrong choice to make.

You might lose points and deductions if you do so, and so, you must consider buying your house within the first few months of the year.

It is also important for you to time your buying and selling operations, in order to make the most of it. Some people plan it in such a way that they sell their existing house and buy a new one within a few days' time. This will allow them to maximize their profits. There are also some who will sell and buy on the same day and literally hit jackpot. But if this is not a possibility for you, then you can consider the next option.

Two time

If you are not able to sell and buy a house within a short period of time and urgently need to vacate in order to reduce your taxes, then you can rent a house and shift temporarily while your current house sells. This can be especially important if you are not eligible to own two houses at the same time, as you do not want to get into trouble for it.

In another scenario, if you think you can afford a big fancy house and have enough time on your hands, then you can shuttle between both houses and renovate each, to move into one and sell the other. Doing so will also allow you to avail certain tax benefits.

Joint return

If you and your spouse file a joint return, then you will be able to double the exemption. So it is best to invest in real estate with your spouse or partner, as it will only work to your advantage.

Here is an extract of the law from the IRS website:

You may qualify to exclude up to $500,000 of that gain if you file a joint return with your spouse.

Repeat

Once you buy and move into your new house, you must again repeat the same things that you did with the previous one. You must renovate it and occupy it for two years and then look for another house to move to, and sell the previous one for a hefty price. You must keep up with this loop, as it will help you make huge profits.

Dedication

Lastly, it might seem a bit impossible to do all this every two years but with time, you will find it easy to carry out these operations. Once the money starts to roll in, you will not look back. A little dedication will go a long way in helping you build a massive wealth and give yourself, and your family, a great life.

Andy Anderson

Chapter 8

Buying and Selling Property Abroad

In the previous chapter, we looked at how you can buy and sell property locally, in order to avail tax benefits. But what if you buy property outside your country? Will you be able to avail the same types of tax benefits? Well, let's find out.

Once you start buying and selling houses locally, you will develop the confidence to do it internationally. You will have enough money to fund your foreign purchases; given you carry out your buying and selling business smartly.

Buying properties abroad is a great idea, if you are only a few years away from retiring, as it will give you the opportunity to settle down in the place of your dreams. And in the process, you will be able to save on your taxes.

Most of the tax laws that apply to your local properties will extend to your foreign properties. Depending on how you will use them, you will be able to save hefty amounts on taxes.

Here are the ways in which you can use your foreign properties.

Personal use

If you are using your foreign home for personal use, then you will avail the same tax benefits as you would in the US, for your second home. You can deduct the mortgage interest and up to 100% of the interest that you would pay up to 1.1$ million of debt secured by both your homes with the amount being collective and not individual. You will be able to deduct property tax on your foreign home and if you are to buy another one there, then it will extend to that one as well.

But remember that you must stay put in the house for two years and not merely use it as a vacation home. You can also have your family members (your spouse, siblings, parents, grandparents, children and grandchildren) stay there and it will still qualify as personal use. If you do use it as a vacation home, then the rules will differ. If at any time, you live for less than 15 days, then it will be considered a vacation home. You will, however, still be able to deduct mortgage interest and property taxes.

If you collect a fair rent from any of these members, then it will qualify as a rented property.

Rental purposes

The tax rules for rental income on foreign property are quite different from what it is in the US. Depending on the type of rent agreement, it can be divided in the following three ways.

•   Renting it out for 14 days or less: if you rent out the property for 14 days or less in 1 year, then you need not report the rental income to the IRS. So even if you charge 10,000$ a night for a luxurious condo in an exotic island, you will still be able to get away with it. Adding to it will be your option to deduct the mortgage interest and property taxes, which will only help you, make the most of your earned money.

•   Renting it out for 15 days or more and using it for 14 days or less: in this case, the IRS will consider it to be a rental property and you must report all the income that you receive in terms of rent. However, you will be able to deduct all your expenses such as advertising expenses, insurance premiums, mortgage interests, property taxes etc. just like you would with your local rental property.

•   Using property for more than 14 days and 10% of those days was rented: in this case, it will be considered as property for personal use. All the same rules will apply to such a property and will prevent you from deducting rental expenses and losses. You can deduct mortgage interest and property taxes.

As is apparent, it can get a bit complex when it comes to the tax laws that are levied on foreign properties, if you wish to use for rental purposes.

Selling the property

The same tax laws apply to selling your foreign house, as they would for a local property. Depending on whether you lived there for a total of 2 years out of the last 5, you will be able to exclude up to 250,000$ of capital gains and up to 500,000$ for a joint return with your spouse, from the sale.

Depreciation

The depreciation laws defer between local and foreign properties. Local properties are depreciated over a period of 27.5 years, whereas, foreign properties are depreciated over a period of 40 years. This is an advantage as you will be able to sell your property for a higher value. Say for example you own two properties with one being in the US and the other being abroad and both are worth 100,000$. Your annual depreciation value for your US property will come up to 3,636$ and the foreign property will come up to 2,500$. So basically, you can buy and sell properties abroad just as you would locally and earn a lot of tax-free money that you can enjoy.

Andy Anderson

Chapter 9

Best Types of Houses to Buy

In the previous chapter, we looked at the best way in which you can keep the property buying and selling going, both nationally and internationally, in order to make good profits and in this one, I will run you through the best types of houses that you can buy and sell to help you pay zero taxes. Even as you go from being a normal, layman real estate investor to a real estate agent, you can keep these things in mind – they will definitely come in handy later!

Distress sales

There can be no better deal for you than to find a house through a distress sale. Distress sales are those where the owner will be in a hurry to sell the house and willing to sell it for a price much lower than the actual value of the house. This will allow you to buy the house at a cheap price and if you are lucky, it will be in great condition. Once you complete two years in the house, you can dispose it off for a high price and make a big profit out of it. For this to happen, you will have to scour around your area, from time to time, and also look at ads that are published online. You must also keep in touch with an estate agent who will tell you about a good house. Remember that such houses are never advertised in a big way and you have to look for them in all the smallest of places like random newspaper ads.

Bad shape

Look for houses that are in a bad shape and need to be fixed. You will be able to get the house for a cheaper price and fixing it up will allow you to deduct the money from your income. People generally look for houses that need painting, fixture replacement and floor replacement, as they make for good houses to renovate. As was mentioned earlier, it is important that you look for something that needs a fair bit of renovation like fixing a major problem. However, don't settle for something that is in extremely bad shape as you might end up buying property that needs a lot of fixing up. It is best that you personally inspect every detail of the house before you make your final purchase.

Foreclosed homes

Buying houses at foreclosures and auctions will help you get a good deal. Foreclosed houses are those, that are sold by financial institutions such as banks and money lending companies, in order to make back whatever that they had lent. They will not look for profits and so; you will be able to buy the house at the original price, which will be much lesser than the market trending price. Auctioneers generally auction off old houses for people who wish to dispose off their property and if the starting bid of the house is quite low, then you might be able to get the house for a cheap price.

FSBOs

"For sale by owner" houses are a good choice, as you will get to avoid paying estate agent fees. Another advantage is that you can try and bargain with the owner, something that might not be possible with the agent. You can look up on the Internet for houses that are advertised by the owners themselves and find yourself a good deal. You will also find these if you look out for "for sale" signboards. These are indicative that the owner is himself advertising it and you stand a chance at getting it at a good price.

REIAs

You can decide to become a member of the real estate investors association, as it will allow you to be informed of all the trending rates for houses and have access to properties that are up for sale.

Family properties

Buying property from family members will allow you to get them at discounted prices. Even if it is just a small discount, you will be able to make a good profit from it, when you decide to sell it later. Be on the look out for any family member that is ready to sell their house. Inform all that you will be interested in it and should be asked first.

Foreign properties

As was seen in the previous chapter, you will be able to make huge profits out of owning a foreign property. Pretty much the same criteria apply when it comes to looking for a good deal, abroad. You can hire someone to look for a property for you and then close the deal.

These form the various types of properties that you can consider, when you wish to invest in real estate for tax benefits

.

Chapter 10
Obstacles To Consider Along The Way

Investing in real estate properties will help you pay zero taxes and make huge profits, but there can be a few obstacles in the way, which you must deal with, in order to find great success.

Issues with local properties

Depreciation

One downfall of buying a house and trying to sell it after 2 or 5 years is that, the value of the house would have depreciated. This will affect your profits to a large extent. The IRS calculates the depreciation over a 27.5-year period. Now suppose you bought a house for 275,000$ and it was a price that was below market value. Over time, owing to wear and tear and visible changes inside and outside the house, the value of the house might depreciate by 40%. So, if you are to command a price of 800,000$ for it, then you will only get 300,000$ for it after depreciation, and your profit will amount to 205,000$. This depreciation will, however, vary depending on how well the house has been maintained. If the house is still in great shape, then the depreciation value may come down to 20% and your profit will surmount to 365,000$.

You can then go on to buy a house for 300,000, and be left with a profit of 65,000$, which is not taxable. By investing this money into buying another property, you will help avoid paying the recapture tax, and this will only work to your benefit.

Emergencies

Sometimes, unforeseen events might force you to vacate your house before you hit the 2-year mark. Things like a natural calamity or death/ illness of a near and dear one might cause you to sell your house earlier than expected, to relocate to another place. In such cases, you will not be able to fulfill your desire to make a profit by selling it at a high price and buying a new one at a low price. However, you can make a family member occupy the house and complete 2 years of residence and return to carry forward your enterprise.

Attachment

Many times, people get attached to their house and find it difficult to move out. This can be, especially, apparent amongst those who live in houses for more than 4 years, as they would have well settled into their neighborhood.

This can be a big problem and so, many people make up their mind to not fall in love with a place and move at as soon as the 2 years are up. Some people renovate their houses only a little and claim tax benefits instead of splurging on it to make it posh. However, if the renovations are only minimal, then the person might have difficulty selling the house.

Personal problems

Personal problems such as divorce or parting ways with a partner can create problems for your property plans. If your divorce coincides with your plans to sell or buy your property and your partner owns half of it and is not interested in selling, then you can be in trouble. The best thing to do in order to avoid this is to make an official pact with your partner to do things that will be in the best interest of both parties, should the two of you ever decide to part ways.

Issues with foreign properties

Difficulty buying and selling

One of the biggest problems of buying a house in a foreign location is that, it can get quite difficult to look for good deals.

You cannot be based in Miami and look for the best deal on a house in Italy. It will get tough to manage the various involved elements and it will be no less difficult to sell the property. The best solution for this is to either hire someone to deal for you in the foreign country or have a relative, located there, look at your business. Doing so will only help you score the best deals.

Difficulty maintaining

Just as with buying and selling a foreign property, it might be difficult to supervise and assess the condition of the house from time to time. For example: if you decide to rent the house for 5,000$ and allow only 4 people to stay and one day find out that 8 of them have occupied the house, then you will undergo a loss. The best thing to do is to, again, have a relative take care of matters or appoint an agent to do it for you. But that will cost you.

Double taxation

You will have to steer clear of double taxation if you wish to make a large profit out of your foreign property. You will have to pay both your government and the other country's government money, if you use the property for rental purposes. But you can prevent double taxation by taking a tax credit on your US tax returns for any taxes that you might have paid to the foreign country's government in connection with your net rental income. But remember that you cannot claim credit for more than the amount that you pay in the US for the rental income, after all expenses have been deducted. This is the exact reason why people buy houses in countries where the property tax is low.

Culture difference

You might have a problem knowing what the locals will like in terms of properties. Maybe they like a certain type of property but you might end up buying something that is not to the local's taste. You will end up undergoing a loss and might have to make a lot of trips back and forth, which is a waste of time and money.

These can be some of the pitfalls that might come your way when you decide to buy and sell property to evade tax and must take appropriate measures to avoid them.

With that, we come to the end of the real estate guide for the individual investor who wants to use real estate to make money. By the time you have managed to accomplish all of this, learnt to avoid over paying your taxes, you already well versed in the real estate industry and can easily branch out into being a real estate agent if you want. It is the next logical step, in fact – you invested initially in real estate, then you learnt to play the tax laws to your benefit and now, you can build your own wealthy empire from setting up a real estate business that you can run out of your own home office.

In the next couple of chapters, I have given you quick steps and strategies you can follow to become successful, not only as an individual real estate investor, but an actual real estate agent.

Chapter 11
Quick Strategies to Get You Started in Real Estate

As I said previously, the real estate business is one of the most lucrative businesses out there, which can help you earn a lot of money and live in the lap of luxury all your life. However, you cannot just jump into the business with no prior knowledge of how it runs – you will end up making poor decisions and losing what money you do have. Don't panic, though! In this chapter, I am going to give you some quick strategies you can follow when you are just beginning in the real estate world. Employ these when you are buying, selling or renting a place, and they will definitely help you! Also, these are rather general principles that even the individual investor can follow, so be sure to read through them properly!

Bargain like your life depends on it

Learn to haggle like a crazy person. As is obvious, when you are buying property, the costs sky rocket, especially in today's world, where the value of land tends to appreciate more often than not. In fact, the trend on behalf of the sellers themselves is to have the prices cranked up, simply so that they can allow their prospective buyers a little leeway when it comes to bargaining. That just means that they are willing to fight you for a price that both of you can agree on; they are ready and waiting for you to bargain. So, no matter how desperate you are to buy a particular piece of property, do not hesitate to bargain for it – the buyers *expect* it, and it lends you a subtle credibility that you cannot win otherwise.

To begin with, look around the area where the property you want buy is situated in. Check out the prices and do your market research. See what the general cost is and then arrive at a fixed price that you think will be ideal for that property in that area. Remember to take into account the external factors; for instance, if it is a property that is in the suburbs, access to the city is something you may want to consider. A house closer to the subway will definitely be worth more than one that is far off. So look at such factors when you try to arrive at a worthy price.

When it comes to the actual bargaining, start your haggling by quoting a sum that is 10% lesser than the amount you actually plan to pay for it. Obviously, your seller will not agree – do not back down. The secret to any good bargain is to be absolutely confident and self-possessed, so do not allow yourself to be intimidated by your seller and continue to stress on the reduced amount you want to pay.

The other party will attempt to raise it, and after you have had a bit of a back-and-forth to establish your common ground, raise your amount and quote a sum that is 5% less than your actual price. Once again, the seller is going to protest, and once again, you are going to remain calm and confident. Keep it going for a little while, and ultimately, the seller will compromise and you will be able to pay just the amount you wanted to buy the property for.

Keep in mind – nobody is willing to take anything less than what they think they deserve. Money is important to everybody, which means that the seller is going to be willing to fight you tooth and nail to get his maximum profit from you. Whether you plan to keep the property or flip it later, it does not matter – quote your budget and refuse to budge. Dig in your heels and remain calm; the seller will eventually meet you halfway and you will be able to stroke up a deal. Remember though, if you are unprepared, there is a good chance you will be blindsided by the seller. He is going to have a number of tricks up his sleeve, so be ready for anything. Do your research and make sure you go to the meeting absolutely ready.

Understand and undertake 'Flipping'

'Flipping' is one of the most important and effective practices you can employ as a real estate agent. This entails the buying and selling of the property almost simultaneously; as you buy the house, you are also making arrangements to sell it immediately, sometimes even before you own it completely. Obviously, as with any business venture, the idea is to make a profit, so you will need to be careful while selecting the property you want to flip.

Look for a house that is in good condition and will not need repairs or any such thing. Also make sure that the seller is giving you a price that is below the trending price; the whole idea of this is to keep your costs at a low by taking away the renovation aspect of things. You will not have to spend much money on the house, and you can make a profit from your selling price alone, since you will be able to sell the property as it is, without additional costs.

Quick reminder – you cannot rent out the house. The idea of flipping is to buy it and sell it immediately, so the moment you close the deal, begin haggling your prospective buyer for a better price to sell at. Ideally, you should have already found a buyer even before the property was fully yours.

The advantage in this deal is obviously the lesser costs. You can make profits at a very quick pace, and your loss margin is relatively less. Generally, the trend is to resell the house at a profit margin of around 15-20%, so stick to that and you will be able to make a lot of money in flipping houses!

Know when to 'buy and hold'

You saw one type of deal, where you buy and sell a house immediately. Obviously, the next type of deal is one where you buy property and hold it before you sell it. This is the exact opposite f flipping, where you do not immediately resell. Instead, you wait for the value of the property to appreciate, and after it has crossed a good margin, you can start looking for potential buyers to buy the property. The general trend is to wait until the value of the house goes up by more than 15%, so follow that rule of thumb, and you will earn quite a bit of money!

The advantage and disadvantage of the *'buy and hold'* technique – depending on perspective and your financial situation – is that you have time to renovate the property. Obviously, it is going to add to your initial costs, unlike with flipping. But that is the precise reason why this is a good idea; because you renovate the place, you add more value to it! New additions can definitely increase the selling price later, so set aside some of your capital for the express purpose of buying and holding property instead of flipping.

Now, obviously, there are some ground rules when choosing the house you are going to buy. Your initial investment cannot be very big; you need to have money to be able to renovate and spruce up the place as well. So look for property that specifically undervalued. Look around the market; too often, there are houses flying under the radar that, if renovated, have the potential to increase exponentially in their value. Once again, take the external and internal factors into consideration, and when you make the sale, pitch it properly. Restoration/renovation of the property may be costly, but it will certainly be worth it if you have chosen the right kind of house in the right kind of area.

Here is a quick tip – this kind of buying, renovating and selling houses is best for huge profits if the houses chosen are from developing localities, perhaps centered around an industry or so. These localities are still growing, so naturally, the value of any property in these places will only appreciate. Buy the house when the area is in its growth stage; renovate it – your costs will be lower than you expect, since the area is still under development! Wait until the growth stage reaches its saturation and then start looking out for potential buyers. You will make a huge profit, despite the renovation/restoration costs!

Work out Hybrid deals

The third type of deal is a mix of the previous two – a combination of flipping and buying and holding. Essentially, you buy a house, renovate it for a small price and then rent it out, following which you sell it at a much higher price. Obviously, you are not going to sell it until you have recovered all the costs of restoration from your rent, which means that your profit margin is going to be even higher than before!

In this situation, the types of houses you want to go in for are those properties, which require a fair bit of work. Look out for places, which have the potential to appreciate if they are renovated well. Go hybrid on those houses, which just require that little bit of work to really make a sale.

Quick tip to keep in mind – when you rent out your house, make sure your tenant knows that you are going to sell the house later and have a contract prepared if you are going to ask him to share the renovation costs. Having your tenant repair your house for you reduces your own investment; it is a very lucrative option and one that goes a long way towards increasing your profit!

Sub-let

This is another very important and effective real estate strategy. You acquire property on a lease or a rent basis and then sublet it to a tenant of your own at a higher rate than the amount you are paying for it.

Now what you have to keep in mind while subletting your property is that the margin between the rent you are paying and the rent you are receiving has to be quite a substantial amount. A mere couple of hundred dollars is not going to cut it; you need to make a proper profit, which is why it is a very god idea to treat your new house as a commercial outlet.

For instance, if it is a condo that you are renting, try to make arrangements to have it converted into a bachelor pad and bring in more than a single tenant. Or if you are renting a whole building, you could have whole floors converted into offices for other small companies who want to rent office spaces. Simultaneously subletting houses and buildings instead of just a single house or apartment will make you a huge profit.

Of course, the downside is that you essentially play the middleman between the tenants and the actual owners of the property. You may have to consult the owners for changes you want to make to the houses, and there may be legal contracts and policies you will have to sign and adhere to. Keep all those factors in mind when you choose sublet.

Andy Anderson

Chapter 12
Estate Qualifications To Keep In Mind While Buying Property

Now when you get into the real estate business, the first thing you must consider is what property to buy. Obviously, you cannot just randomly purchase houses and try to sell them; you will definitely end up in loss. Selecting property to invest in and then reap rewards off of is a skill that has to be developed, but it will definitely go a long way in earning you a rich profit!

Here are some of the things you need to take into consideration when you start buying property. Keep them in mind, and you will do just fine! A lot of these pointers apply to both the real estate agent as well as the individual – I may have already mentioned them earlier too. Bear with me; they are important things to consider, so read through them carefully before you begin spending your money!

Location Assessment

Without a doubt, the most important aspect of choosing property in real estate is the location. Nobody wants to live in a dump, after all – make sure that the place you choose to buy your house in is a nice locale. Choose a picturesque setting for it; a house on the seaside or a house by the mountains maybe a cliché, but they have a precedent for sale that most other properties don't. Of course, such houses that generally belong more to paintings than the real world are rare to come by and they are expensive too boot; just make sure that the house you buy has a nice setting, and looks like a home. More often than not, people are attracted by simplicity and elegance, so go in for those qualities than just opulence.

Keep in mind the neighborhood as well, along with your own target audience. For instance, a family of four may prefer the American Dream Home with a white picket fence in the suburbs, but single bachelors may want a condo on a high rise building in the middle of the city. Scope out the area before you decide to invest in property there; run a quick check on all the neighbors of your potential buyers so that you are armed with information when you make your sales pitch.

Keep an eye out for the other important facilities like malls, schools, hospitals, etc. the closer the property is to these amenities, the more its value shoots up. In fact, a smaller house with access to all of these may sell for twice the rate of a big property without access.

At the end of it, make sure you pick a house that falls in line with the dream home of your target audience. As a real estate agent, your idea is to sell property that people want for a particular purpose; be aware of that purpose before you choose the house you want to buy and then flip or renovate.

Price Assessment

Now that you have chosen the place where you want to make your investment, the next most important decision you have to make is how much you want to invest in the first place. Too often, people end up paying more money that is necessary to buy a particular piece of property, blowing huge holes in their pockets. Instead, a little bit of research will definitely save you a couple grand, and you will still be able to get the property that falls into your parameters.

There are no hard and fast rules to this kind of research work. The simplest pointers to keep in mind are these – age of the house, its depreciation value and the location are three factors that affect the price of any house. Scope out the different localities you want to invest in and then do a comparison and a cross referencing to see which properties you can afford to buy. Also decide if you want to flip the houses or renovate them; unless you know the purpose for which you are buying property, you cannot decide which house to buy.

If you do plan on renovating a house, make sure you can afford to spend the money. Turning a cheap dump into a multi-million dollar condo sounds like an amazing thing to do, but it can be a little too ambitious and not very cost-effective. You have to account for your expenses and still make a tidy profit, so keep your overall budget in mind before you choose any house to invest in!

Value Assessment

Buying property is all about assessing the value of a house. This is actually the extension of the previous idea; you need to decide if the property you want to buy is worth the money you are going to be spending on it. Let me give you an example. Suppose you have your eye on a big house with a couple of hills in the background, making it look picturesque. Now you could buy such a property, renovate it and have it look gorgeous – and still, you may not be able to find a proper buyer for it. Dig a little deeper, and you will find that the value of the house is nowhere close to the amount of money you spent on it; it could be that it is too far away from the nearest town and therefore the basic amenities. It could be that the idea of living in such isolation throughout the year is not a good sales pitch; you might have to rent it out on a seasonal basis instead, perhaps as a vacation cottage. If that is what you have to do, you may find that you have spent extra money on the renovations and even the purchase itself, leading to a loss instead of a profit.

Ultimately, you must assess the true value of the property you are buying. Do a thorough research on all internal and external factors, from the locality to the purpose of buying. Ask yourself questions like these – why am I buying this place? What is my budget and how much can I afford to spend on it? Will I be able to make a sale with what I have or will have to change my sales pitch? If yes, then how much is that going to cost me?

Also look out for overpriced houses. If you can haggle the price down and manage to keep it within your budget – then go ahead! But if it is going to cost you much more than what its true value is, then step back. Keep in mind – assessing the true worth of a property is as dependent on external factors as it is the property itself, so be careful before spending your hard-earned money on any purchase!

Age/condition Assessment

Now here come the specifics of the property in question itself. So far, we looked at external factors like the locale and the neighborhood; now, let us take a look into the building that you want to buy. Obviously, the parameters would have to be rated according to the age of the building and the condition it is in.

The older a building, the more difficult maintenance of it becomes. If you do buy an old house, make sure that you do not overspend; you may have to save the money for renovations, from rewiring the plumbing to whipping the garden back into shape.

There are other hiccups in buying old property; buyers will want to take it from you at a lesser price than what you want to sell it at, even if the renovations have been spot on. Make sure that you can sell the house at a profit if you do choose to buy such a building. They may also have an issue with the type of renovating you wish to do. It maybe a better idea to buy old buildings only when a client specifically asks for it, or if you have a potential buyer already lined up.

And if the building is new, then ensure that it is in good working condition and that you will not have to pay for extra fixes. Buyers prefer new and well-maintained property; so keep that in mind before you scout any houses you want to invest in. Ultimately, remember, you have a budget and you need to make a profit, so buy any houses that fall into those parameters.

History Assessment

Now, the value of the property is based not just on the building itself, but the history behind it as well. This could be an external history, such as a crime filled locale, in which case, it might be a better idea to buy and hold the house while the reputation of the area slowly improves.

But sometimes, a house will come along with a wonderful history that you can use as your sales pitch. The perception of the public has a definite influence on the property you are buying and/or selling – if the house's history is rife with uncomfortable stories like hauntings or crimes, and then its value will depreciate. You will have to buy and hold it for a while, or it maybe a better idea to not buy it at all. On the other hand, sometimes, the history is good – like a war hero's old home, or the birth of an eminent personality – which makes the value of the house much more than its actual price. In those cases, it might be better to flip the houses as soon as you get it.

Whatever the situation, be smart and appraise the house from all angles before you decide to invest in it. Make a proper plan regarding its future; if you are going to hold it, see how much the holding costs – from renovation to maintenance – is going to be and if it is going to be worth it in the end. If not, then it might be a better idea to not buy the place. Just don't take a house at its face value; history changes perspective, even if it has no bearing on the present itself, so keep that in mind when you buy property!

Chapter 13
5 Quick Deal Makers

So far, we have looked into the things you need to keep in mind when you buy property. Now in this chapter, I am going to give you 5 quick ways that you can get good deals on any real estate you wish to invest in. Following these does not mean that you will always be successful, but they certainly improve your chances to make a tidy profit!

Attend Auctions

Auctions are a real estate agent's double-edged sword – they can be as profitable as they can a way to quick loss. At an auction, you are in control of the sale and you can choose to buy or not to buy the property on sale. You have the chance to outbid your competitor – but don't get carried away! Auctions tend to be racy and fast-paced, and the auctioneers play up the emotions of the buyers to manage a good sale. Bear in mind the property's actual, true value as well as your own budget before you buy it.

The simplest way of getting the best out of auction sale is to identify the true value of the property you are bidding on and then enter the auction with a budget limit that is 10% above that value. Keep that as your last limit; if your competitor is bidding more than that, it is good idea to let the sale go, since it is definitely not worth that much money. Even if you add the renovation costs to it, it is doubtful that it will be a profitable sale later.

Start your own bidding at a value that is 5% above the true worth and haggle up to 10%. Do not go beyond that. Also, keep in mind the other bidders' strategies; if you know what they are, they alter your own accordingly to make sure you get the best deal. Obviously, such knowledge is hard to come by, so stick to this rule of thumb, and you will be able to get some really good deals at auction sales!

Distress Sales

Distress sales are a dream come true for any realtor. As the name suggests, the owner is basically desperate to rid himself of the house, or building, and will be willing to sell it at a much lower price than its true value. We already spoke about this earlier, but to reiterate, the owner's priority is the quick disposal of the property and/or a fast realization of consideration. He is not interested in haggling the prices to make that extra grand.

Without a doubt, this is a situation you need to pounce on. Capitalize on this opportunity and buy such houses immediately; you will definitely be able to make a profit, considering the low cost price you are going to pay for it. The buy and hold option may be an even better idea in this case; you can spend the extra money from the purchase to renovate the house and sell it at an even bigger profit, thanks to the new additions. The value of the property may also appreciate, adding to your profit margin by a large extent, given the low price you paid to buy the house.

Before you make the purchase though, do identify why the owner wants to sell the house so quickly. If it is a sound reason – such as a need for quick cash, or moving to another country – then take the deal without hesitation and capitalize on the chance to make a huge profit. However, if it is because of something more sinister, like a crime having taken place within the house, then step back and think about it twice before you make the purchase. Even then, a little bit of advertising could turn the perception of the property around to help you hit that high profit margin. Calculate all the factors before you make the purchase.

Foreclosures

Foreclosures are a brilliant way to buy good property at fairly discounted rates. The creditor wants only to get back the money that was owed to him – he is generally not interested in haggling for extra profit, which means that the house will be available for sale at a highly discounted price. Buying it and then flipping will help you get a huge profit margin that you would be able to achieve otherwise.

Let me give you an example. Supposing a person – say, Sam – buys a house, for which he pays 10% out of his own savings and takes out a loan for the rest of the amount. Out of the 90% he borrowed, he is able to pay only 5% and has to forfeit the house in the end. The creditor will foreclose the property and attempt to sell it, but his effort is only to regain the 85% that is owed to him. He is not bothered about the true worth of the property.

Inevitably, he will end up selling it at a discounted price. He needs only 85% of the money back, which means that the house is going to cost much less than its actual value. As a real estate agent, you should capitalize on such an opportunity immediately – given that it is a creditor who is closing the sale, chances are that the property is in really good condition. Flipping the purchase will earn you a huge profit.

Beware though – most foreclosures are not made public knowledge. You will have to be aware of what is happening in the neighborhood to be able to capitalize on one, so keep yourself plugged into the grapevine and regularly scout your locales to do so!

Outright Sale

Outright sales are expensive deals, but they are a good deal to make in the long run. There are no special arrangements in outright sales, and you will have to pay the full amount without any bargaining for lowered prices. The deal is simple – pay, buy and then keep the house.

Since you cannot haggle for prices, it may be possible that you do not have sufficient funds to afford the property. In such cases, look for loans and do not be shy about approaching creditors. Once the property is yours, do not flip it; a good idea is to wait until the house appreciates and increases in value to make a resale and therefore, a good profit. Renting it out is also a good option – it will allow you to earn some of the money back to repay your creditors, while you wait for the property's value to increase to make a proper profit.

As always, keep in mind the external factors like locale and access when you buy the house. Look at all your options before you make the purchase; do comparative studies and enough market research to make sure you will make a profit. The amount of money you will spend on the initial investment is not going to be small – ensure that it is going to be worth it and give you proper returns before you go ahead with the purchase.

Buy-move-sell

For the layman, this will not even seem like a real estate agent's strategy to sell houses. As the name suggests, this a deal maker that implies buying a house, moving into it for a couple of years and then sell it much later. Obviously, you cannot do this with every property you want to deal in, but it is a good idea in times of recession when people do not want to invest in property at all.

This usually works when you want to exercise the buy and hold option but do not want to lease it out to a tenant. Move in yourself and then work around the house to see what all needs to be done; it gives you an advantage when you are trying to sell it out later. As some one who has lived there yourself, your sales pitch will be much more meaningful and confident and you can give your potential buyer the best of the property, since you have already experienced it for yourself.

Essentially, this is a good idea when you move from being an individual investor to beginning your own real estate business.

Obviously, you will have to wait for a while until the true value of the property has gone up and beyond what you bought the place for. Give yourself a profit margin to wait; once it crosses that margin, you can start thinking about selling the property.

Another option is to have a relative or a friend move in instead of you. Basically, this strategy is to ensure that the house does not become dilapidated or dirty while you await its appreciation and the best way of doing that is to ensure human inhabitation. Renting out may not be a good idea for everyone, but having a relative or a friend substitute will definitely fulfill your needs while you wait for the house's value to go up enough for you to make a good, tidy sum of profit. You can trust them to look after the house the way you would yourself, and if need be, you can even charge them a discounted rent. That way, you can get rid of any uneasiness of renting out to a stranger, while still earning a quick buck.

Andy Anderson

Chapter 14
The *Don'ts* Of Real Estate

Up until now, I have told you about some the top strategies you can adopt that will help you land the best deals and the best prices. But as with every field, there are certain things you must not do – these are the don'ts of real estate and you should adhere to them as much as possible, so that you do not end up losing money.

Don't No.1 - Don't be over or under confident

As with any industry, overconfidence will be the key to your downfall. You cannot be the most successful person in real estate, or the richest. There is always someone out there who is better at bargaining than you, who is richer than you or who is much better connected than you are. Real estate investment can be like chess; you have to plan your moves well in advance, and make sure you are not so overconfident that you have no contingency plans in place in case of loss.

The best part of real estate investment is that it does not have to be the main source of your income. It can be an additional business that pools in some extra cash – particularly for the individual, who may hold a 9-5 job, and rent out a property to a family because he owns it and wants some extra money. On the other hand, if you do want to build an empire of wealth based on the real estate business, then you are going to have to work hard; success does not come easy. You will face a number of ups and downs and you may not always come out on top. Be determined and persevere – you will definitely make it big if you keep trying! Don't lose your confidence because you lost one or two sales; we all make mistakes and we all have to learn from them to become better!

A good idea for those who want to go straight into the real estate business is to take up an internship at a well-known firm. That way you will understand the intricacies of the industry and will be able to branch out on your own later, making slow but steady progress.

Do not assess an owner/ agent based on how he or she looks. You have nothing to do with it and you might end up losing out on a great deal just because you were too busy judging someone. Try and remain as neutral as possible. Your primary focus should be on the house and you must not get distracted by anything else.

Don't No.2 - Don't expect quick results

As with any proper business venture, you cannot go from being a layman to Bill Gates overnight. Real estate takes hard work and time to amount to anything worth something, so be patient and persevere.

There are some people who remain extremely impatient and end up making a mistake and don't even realize it. They again make a mistake and think it is the right thing to do. That is where the change needs to come in. You have to remain patient and have faith in yourself. No property is going to run away from you just because you are going a little slow. Everything should go at a regular pace. Don't hurry any part of the buying, selling or renting processes. Have an ideal time frame in your mind and follow the plan accordingly.

Investments take time to reap returns. For instance, if you have purchased a property in an area where the growth potential is slowly developing, it is a better idea to wait patiently until the saturation point is fulfilled before you sell it. If you make a hurried decision to sell it off earlier than you should, you will end up losing those couple thousand dollars more that you could have earned if you had simply waited for the value of the property to automatically appreciate.

Think of it as a plant that you have sown and how it will take time for it to produce fruits. You need to wait for it to grow in value over a certain period of time. Until such time, you must remain patient.

The other option is to flip the property; the problem with this is that you may have to buy and flip a number of houses back to back to earn yourself a substantial amount of money.

Remember, it will take you at least 3-4 years to be able to establish yourself as a successful real estate agent or investor. It will take hard work and determination; you will have to do proper market research to keep yourself up to date with the current market trends. You cannot rush into making purchases or sales – it will take time to understand when, where and how you should invest and how you can reap proper rewards from it. And remember, even if you make mistakes that prove costly – don't give up! Do not let one or two experiences keep you away from the world of business; risk is a part of it and you will have to accept that when you make your first investment itself!

Don't No.3 – Don't Miscalculate

This is one of the most obvious and most important things to keep in mind when making real estate investments, both as a real estate agent and as an individual. You cannot afford to overpay or sell at an underpriced rate – you will be cheated out of your money. Always get the math right, particularly if you are going to be investing in huge properties like commercial real estate for other establishments.

Have some software installed that will allow you to keep tabs on how much you have invested in what properties. You could also maintain a journal instead, if you are old school and prefer not to trust modern technology.

Keep a sharp eye on the balance between your cash inflow and outflow. If the former is less than the latter, you are running at a definite loss and you may have to step back and see where you are losing the money and how you can rectify the situation.

Here is another quick accounting tip to keep in mind – never count the money that has not been credited to your account. Whether it is rent from a tenant that is due or it is the money accrued from a sale, regard the unpaid amount as a debt and wait till you receive the cash to add it to your books.

If accounting proves too difficult for you, hire an accountant to help you out. In fact, you could even look for cheap options by offering part time jobs to accounting students who will need the experience and have the expertise to help you out!

Of course, as humans, we are bound to make mistakes. If you do end up miscalculating some figures, don't hesitate to tell the other party about it! The sooner you own up, the sooner you can clean up the mess and the lesser the amount of money both you and the other party loses. Try to buy some time to correct your mistake, and try your best to make for the money lost by cutting down on other costs. But *never* ever go ahead without appraising the deal thoroughly and make sure there are no miscalculations before you enter into any venture.

Don't No.4 – Don't over pay taxes

I have already given you a detailed account of how you can avoid overpaying your taxes in the previous chapters, but I will reiterate here once again. Real estate investments have always been seen as the best ways to avoid paying tax, so make full use of the tax benefits available to you as a real estate investor!

Don't worry you don't have to feel guilty about any of it. Many people do it all the time and you won't have to worry about having to evade taxes. In fact, evade is the wrong word to use.

You will rightfully not pay, as it will be deducted from your local government's taxes.

Raising a loan allows you to dodge certain taxes. Buying property just before filing for tax and then selling it off within a few months will also allow you save yourself a couple of thousand dollars on tax. Do it on a yearly basis and you will be able to save a lot of money!

Remember though, avoid taxes does not mean dodging the authorities or doing illegal things. What we are doing is availing of the benefits that the government itself is offering, albeit in a roundabout manner. Keep to the legal side of things, and play around with what you can to earn and save money, but do not allow yourself to get into anything shady!

Don't No.5 – Don't be an introvert!

This is as true of any business as it is of real estate. When it comes to being an investor, you cannot afford to be an introvert and make no connections. The stronger your networking skills, the more lucrative the deals you make will be. You need to be plugged into the grapevine and know when and where there are good opportunities to be able to capitalize on them.

Join various real estate communities and attend the agent meetings. Subscribe to real estate magazines and keep yourself up to date with the current trends in the market. And most importantly, go to property fairs, where you can get yourself noticed! Do not shy away from making a splash or letting yourself be known – even if you do not make purchases or sales there, just letting everybody know who you are and what you are capable of will go a long way in helping you establish strong connections that will make you good money.

In the real estate business, you yourself are as much the product as your properties are. You need to come out as a suave, trust worthy and respectable real estate agent or people will think twice about coming to you. Market yourself well – I don't mean boast about yourself or tot your own horn, but be unapologetic about your skills and strengths and let the world know how good you are so that they can approach you for anything.

Don't No. 6 - Don't get over friendly

In the previous segment we saw why you should not be an introvert when it comes to finding the right property. On the other hand, you must not be an extrovert either! This means that being too friendly will only cause you to make mistakes. If you are planning on buying a house then that should be your main motive and you must not head out to make friends. After all, you have to do whatever it takes to do get a good house at the right price and that is only possible if you maintain professional relationships with the different people you brush shoulders with. Don't get over enthusiastic and start acting like you know them from long before and are interested in being their good friend. You have to focus on nothing but the property.

Don't know. 7- Don't miscalculate

Never have just a rough estimate of anything. You have to be absolutely sure of everything before making an investment. If you end up miscalculating then you will pay more than what you actually should be paying. You should try and have a calculator handy where you can punch in the numbers and make the calculations. Those that are not able to do the math easily can always remain in touch with their accountants. You must take their advice on everything and ensure that you are the right thing. You have to remain firm on your agenda and do everything right in order to make the most of your investments.

General tips on investing

Remember that real estate investments are like conducting a business. You must immerse yourself into it fully and treat it like a business venture. Just like you would start with a business plan, you must similarly come up with an investment plan. This plan should incorporate all that you wish to attain from your investment and mark out your journey.

When you wish to invest in real estate, you must check your credit report. You can order it online. It is important that you have a clean record if you wish to avoid any problems in your investment. If there are any errors in the report then you must have it rectified at the earliest.

When you borrow a loan for your investment, it is best that you choose one that comes with a short repayment period. If you keep stretching it then you will end up paying more than what you really should be paying. Also look for a bank that will provide you a good rate of interest.

Chapter 15
Ideal Behavior While Investing in Real Estate

When you go out in the world to buy your ideal property there will be thousands of things that will be swarming your mind. This is especially true for people who are trying to buy their first property. It is really common to have this feeling that you will never be able to buy a good enough piece of property for yourself. You don't have to worry though; this chapter will give you a comprehensive but brief guide regarding the kind of behavior you need to showcase to the world when you go out to buy a house for yourself. There are a lot of options out there regarding the type of houses that you can buy and that can be very confusing.

It is obvious that you might have a lot of things on your mind and have a picture of the ideal house that you want to buy. Even so, it is very difficult to find that exact house that is within your budget. The real estate agent simply wants to fill his pockets and might even mislead you. So, when you go out to buy your house do not let anyone influence you at all, instead you have to be sure about the kind of property that you want and simply go for it. Imagine your ideal house again and again in your mind and do not let go of that dream, this dream will sustain you for the rest of the day and you won't give in to the interests of others.

So, if this is your first time buying a property or the second time, the following tips will depict the kind of ideal behavior that you need to show:

Be Adamant

Property is not something that you just go out to buy spontaneously. Putting resources into a property is a deep-rooted investment that will take control of your monetary future and not just a simple, buy and get rich plan. You will have to be strong if you want to buy the ideal property for yourself. Buying a property can be very confusing and you will probably commit a lot of errors. There are numerous ways in which you can wrong while trying to buy a property. You must always make a plan and go after it. Don't think of things like it is too early or it is too late. Everything will go about the right way as long as you remain determined. Not focusing on the task at hand can cause you to get distracted. That is never the right way to go about it. Be determined to do the right thing and you will be rewarded. You will come up short. The most effective and efficient buyers are the ones who can deal with such shortcomings and transform them into lessons to enhance their aptitudes. This is important because you must not lose hope. If you want to make profits in the long run by investing in real estate you have to play the long game. Be patient, at some point of time the ideal property will show itself. If you buy a property in haste then there is no sure way to know if you will make a profit from it or not. You might actually get a great return on your investment or bear huge losses.

It is not necessary to have a lot of knowledge about Real Estate

A lot of people think about putting their resources into a property however, they simply get hindered with the unlimited measure of data out there. There are so many different types of properties and bank loans and what not available that anyone get hindered in their path to buy a property. It is like saying you have to know all the rules of the game when you go to watch it. That is not true. You can enjoy a game if you know a majority of the rules. You can easily look up online and find the basic rules and the same applies to your real estate business. You can easily look for information online and go after your investment. It will take you mush less time to find your house if you have a plan and go after it determinedly. You real estate agent may seem like the most intelligent person on earth but let me tell you he is not. I am not saying that he is faking his knowledge but it is very difficult to know everything about the world of real estate. There are so many things out there that are related to real estate that it is almost impossible to keep track of everything. The business environment is ever changing and nobody in the world known everything about it. So, you don't have to worry about knowing it all when you go out to invest in real estate rather know only what is necessary and don't spend too much time on research. Get the actual experience by jumping into the world of real estate.

Research is not that important

There are a lot of investors who might be good at many kings of investing and finding the right business opportunities, so they try to jump into the world of real estate thinking that it is easy money and rewards are assured, most of them do not have a lot of experience in this field and are unsure about where to start. Some of the time these financial specialists get fortunate and become wildly however most of the time these speculators fall and fall hard. Try not to be similar to them. Get your work done. Study the specialty you need to put resources into and learn all that you can about that subject. I do not mean that you have to research day and night before you even think about buying a property but it is better to be a little prepared than not being prepared at all. Don't worry you will be able to flip a house easily without having to go through the pains of knowing everything that there is to about real estate. In fact, once you get the hang of it, you will see that your investments are getting easier and you are moving from one house to the other with much ease.

Read as much as you can about Real Estate

If you are reading then of course you need help in buying a property. If you can look for this book then you should look for others as well. There are a lot of books out there than will give you detailed knowledge about the world of real estate. Learn to read a lot. There are many blogs that follow the changes in the business environment, especially business environment related to real estate. These blogs will help you capitalize at the right moment. You have to find the right opportunity for yourself to buy a house. Buying a house at the right time is very important, at a particular time interest rates might be very low and that is extremely helpful. Books have a lot of data in them. You can even study deals that have taken place in the past and learn a lot from them.

Andy Anderson

Try to look for investors in your area

This doesn't intend to spam them with ideas, however just try connecting with other investors. Start hanging out where they hang out. Talk them in to demonstrating to you some of their properties. Most speculators really love to talk about their achievements so permit them to and collect all the good data they can give you. Nearby financial capitalists will have a vastly improved idea about what meets expectations in your area than anybody else. There are many people who know about property but those that locally live in an area tend to have more knowledge about what kind of properties are good. They have a lot of knowledge that can be important if you just try to listen to them.

Get into the world of Real Estate

Literally, you have to hold the bull by the horns. If you want to seem impressive to the other investors, you have to get into the world of real estate by learning about the technical jargon of the real estate world. In the event that you don't have the foggiest idea about the real estate language, you are going to resemble an idiot. Be plain and straightforward but when someone else tries to talk to you in technical terms, you have to talk to them as if you know a lot too. If you try to talk to another investor but don't know the terms of the trade, you'll simply look foolish and show your lack of awareness. Be straightforward on the off chance that you don't know something and don't attempt to be something you are definitely not. Try to let the others start the conversation, this way when they say something you can think of a reply and try to understand the technical terms they used instead of just missing out on them in your own speech.

Look for new ideas

Real estate is a vast subject. As you can see from this book, there is just too much to know about the subject. Your search for knowledge should be endless and you must keep your eyes peeled to know more and more about it. This will only come through only if you make the effort and not by keeping your eyes closed. You have to go after whatever you think is right. You have to learn to change your view about the world. There are some huge investors out there that have a lot of resources while there are some out there who hardly have any and yet can be more successful at times. This is because they worked hard to be more creative. Instead of giving up when faced with the challenge, they went out there and looked for new ideas. If you change your thinking from 'I can't' to 'yes, I can' you will be very successful. All that you need to do to be more successful is look for new ideas and new ways to invest. Just research a bit and look around, you will eventually find the right kind of course of action that will help you to achieve greatness.

Learn to give up on some things

How terrible do you need money related flexibility? On the off chance that you need to utilize property to begin carrying on with the life you've generally imagined you are going to need to give up. You may need to swear off and utilize the cash towards an upfront installment. You may need to move a few times with a specific end goal to develop enough cash flow to start contributing. You may need to figure out how to utilize a paintbrush and do your own particular work. Putting resources into property is the most compensating thing that you can do but however it's not generally simple. There will be years of giving up that you will have to face. You will have to give up on time, cash and a lot of opportunities to get fiscally free. On the off chance that you are searching for a quickly get rich plan look somewhere else. Real estate is very uncertain and you may never know what might happen and when. Return on investment can be high at some point and low on another day. It is better to invest in businesses you are sure about that invest in something that is uncertain. If you can be sure that you will be patient, then you should definitely invest in real estate.

You will need Math

The math included in a property speculation is not school analytics. It is math that even a fifth grader can do and it isn't hard to learn. A simple thing to learn is that when you subtract all the expenses from your incomes you get cash in hand. Something might just cost dollar 2 but in this world most people charge way more for everything, so instead of charging 2 dollars they will charge you twenty dollars. That is the sort of math you have to get the hang of. Try not to be gullible and accept whatever is thrown at you; yet utilize your math to verify whatever numbers are given to you. Excel is a very good application to keep track of all the costs that are given to you and of the expenses that you make. You can even compare the costs of buying different types of properties. When you comprehend the math, don't go amiss from it. Trust it. Try not to let your feelings get included. Property is all about numbers and the best way to feel at investing in a property is by overlooking these numbers and directly jumping to conclusions.

Write everything down

Guides are very important. When you go to a new place, you always consult a guide. Be it guiding yourself through the use of a book or hiring an actual guide to take you around, then why would you venture into the world of real estate without a guide to help you? When you first start thinking about investing, really sit down and make an arrangement to get from where you were to where you need to be. While it can be pretty difficult to stick to the plan that you had made, it will help you because it gives you a direction to work

Don't Aim for something too large

You don't have to purchase a 20-unit loft complex as soon as you start looking at properties. Maybe your first venture will be your first home. Maybe you'll begin with only 50 per cent association on a little house. This is all right. Everyone at some point gets aw e inspired by seeing these big investors making a lot of money from buying houses but you need to know that it is absolutely okay if you do not jump into the world of real estate with a bang. You can start slowly and then develop overtime instead of putting your career in jeopardy by going after something that is out of your reach.

Be respectful of your business

Property is a business so treat it that way. Keep it composed, form frameworks to deal with your life, and try to enhance your effectiveness. The reason such a large number of proprietors get wore out and detest the part is on account of the fact that they do not properly respect the business. You are an entrepreneur and hence the whole real estate thing is your business to deal with it as per the standards that you think suit you the best.

Keep Detailed Financial Records

There are a lot of people that make this mistake and repent for it later on. It is very important to keep records of all the financial transaction that you make. If you do not do this then it might be very difficult for you to know the amount of profits or losses that you are making. You need to understand that real estate is a proper business and hence, needs to be treated that way. A lot of people like to dwell in chaos and have no idea the financial transactions that they are part of. This way the expenses would increase over time and it might be too later for you to recover from the loss.

Don't make Real Estate Your Main Job

Contributing has two confronts: the vocation side and the speculation side. It shouldn't have both. Most people utilize property a lot as of now, however you should genuinely trust that if there were a vocation you loved better then you should do that to simply concentrate on the contributing side. Flipping houses is a vocation's piece "side," as seems to be "wholesaling" and overseeing. Hence, by purchasing cash flowing properties, reinvesting that income into greater and better property, and setting up frameworks to deal with that business, you are making ventures for your own future. There is a simple and small rule that everyone should follow, which means that if you don't have the necessary recourses then you need to work in increasing the quality of your work so that you can sell houses at a higher price because of the quality. On the off chance that your optimal employment is the "profession side" of property then make that your occupation and your venture. Discover whatever employment makes you the happiest and do that, however utilize property as your secondary income generator as it can be really helpful.

Chapter 16
Different Ways to Finance

Regardless of what commercial may persuade, there is no such thing as "free" land. Land is a thing and must be paid for. This chapter is going to show you the ins and outs of different routines you can use to support your land speculations. Such as,

• Understand Real Estate Financing

• Cash Working

• Mortgages

• Portfolios

• Loans

• Self Financing

• Money

• Private Sector Money

- Equity Loans and Credit

- Association

- Loans for Commercial usage

- Other Tools

The importance of Understand Real Estate Financing

The motivation behind this section is to fill you in on the wide range of sorts of land financing that you can use in your land contributing. The distinctive venture vehicles you can take to put resources into land, (for example, single family homes, business land, lofts, and that's only the tip of the iceberg), and a portion of the diverse systems (purchase and hold, flipping, and wholesaling) you can use to profit in land.

At last, the accompanying rundown is in no way, shape or form exhaustive, yet will give you a smart thought of a financing's portion techniques utilized by land speculators to back their land. By having a decent expansive review of these systems, you can consolidate a speculation vehicle, a venture procedure, and a financing technique to handle any land venture.

Money

Do you need to have a considerable measure of cash to put resources into land?

The answer is: no. The more extended answer is not that simple and has a lot of dimensions. There are a lot of real estate projects out there where people don't invest a lot of money. A few arrangements should be possible without utilizing any cash.

Further on you'll locate a few extraordinary methods for financing your land bargains, however in the event that you need more top to bottom data, you should try to consult more and more people so that you can get a lot of data. With that, we should get to an outline of all the financing routines you can use for your land bargains.

Cash Only

Numerous speculators decide to pay all money for a venture property. As indicated by a late joint study, 20 per cent of US financial specialists utilize 100% of their own money to fund their land ventures. To be clear, when financial specialists utilize terms like "All Cash," the fact of the matter is, no "money" is really exchanged. By and large, the purchaser brings a check (typically ensured trusts, for example, a bank clerk's check) to the title organization, and the title organization will compose a check to the vender. Different times, the cash is sent by means of a wire exchange from the bank. This is the simplest type of financing, as there are regularly no entanglements, yet for most speculators (and likely a larger part of new speculators), all money is impossible. Moreover, the result from an all money arrangement won't be the same as when it is not utilized. We should investigate this further by means of an example:

Carl has dollar two hundred thousand to contribute. He can decide to utilize that dollar two hundred thousand to purchase a house that will deliver dollar hundred every month in pay or dollar ne twenty every year. This compares to a 12% degree of profitability.

Carl could likewise rather utilize that two hundred thousand as a 10% up front installment on four comparable homes, each recorded at dollar two hundred thousand. With a dollar eighty thousand contract on each, the income would be around dollar two hundred every month per house, which is dollar fifteen hundred every month each or dollar eighteen thousand every year. This compares to an eighteen per cent rate of profitability - half superior to anything purchasing only one home.

Usually used Mortgages

As should be obvious from the case above, financing your speculation property can create essentially preferred returns over paying all money. Most financial specialists, rather, decide to fund their speculations with a money initial installment and a customary ordinary home loan. Most customary ordinary home loans oblige at least 10% down, yet may stretch out higher to 20-30 per cent for venture properties relying upon the moneylender. Traditional home loans are the most widely recognized sort of home loan utilized by home purchasers and for the most part give the least intrigue rates.

Sources that are based on Portfolio

Customary home loan advances can start from a mixed bag of sources, for example, banks, home loan specialists, and credit unions. Most of the time, these giving sources are not really utilizing their own particular money to finance the credit, yet are getting or obtaining the trusts from another gathering or exchanging the advance to government-upheld foundations, to renew their own stores. Therefore, most loaning organizations must hold fast to an exceptionally strict arrangement of tenets and rules when it comes time to financing a speculation. These strict guidelines can make routine financing hard to get for some, particularly for land speculators and other independently employed borrowers.

Be that as it may, a few banks and credit unions can loan from their own particular supports as well, which makes them a portfolio moneylender. Since the cash is their own, they find themselves able to give more adaptable advance terms and qualifying gauges. This implies that they find themselves able to make advances accessible at any terms satisfactory to them. Customarily a portfolio loan specialist will have stores accessible with less prohibitive capabilities than an ordinary bank.

Most banks or giving establishments don't promote that they are a portfolio moneylender; however, you can discover these people through referrals and systems administration with different financial specialists. You can likewise basically snatch a telephone directory, call every one, and inquire as to whether they are in the business of portfolio lending.

Federal Loans

The Federal Housing Administration (FHA) is a US government program that protects contracts for banks. In the event that you have medical coverage or auto protection, you as of now comprehend the idea: pooling cash to spread the danger for everybody. FHA credits are outlined just for mortgage holders who are going live in the property so you can't utilize a FHA-upheld advance to purchase an unadulterated venture property. In any case, you can exploit the exemption to the standard that permits the FHA-financed home to have up to four separate units. As it were, whether you plan to live in one of the units, you could purchase a duplex, triplex, or fourplex.

The advantage of the FHA credit is the wretched installment prerequisite: at present only 1.5%. This can help kick you off much sooner, since you don't have to set aside 10%. Be that as it may, each gift accompanies a condemnation. While the good installments the FHA offers are extraordinary, the FHA requires an extra installment, called "Private Mortgage Insurance." This "PMI" protection ensures the moneylender and is obliged when the initial installment on a FHA credit is under 10%. The additional PMI installment can make your regularly scheduled installment marginally higher, hence decreasing your income.

Two hundred and three thousand Loans

A sub-set of the FHA credit, the dollar two hundred and three thousand advance is an advance that permits a mortgage holder to buy a house that need some recovery work and gives them the capacity to fund those repairs or changes into the advance itself. Like the typical FHA credit, the two hundred and three thousand advances still take into consideration the down and out installment prerequisite permitted by the FHA. This credit sort is additional material for duplexes, triplexes, and fourplexes, however keeps up the same necessity for being for "proprietor tenants" and accompanies Private Mortgage Insurance requests for advances under 10%.

Self-Financing

Banks or other credit offering establishments, are by all account not the only elements that can fund a property for you. Sometimes, the property's proprietor you need to purchase can really finance the property, and you will basically make your regularly scheduled installment to them instead of a bank. Commonly, the main time a property proprietor will do this for you is when they effectively own the home without a worry in the world, important things is that the vender can't have a current home loan on the property. On the off chance that the vender has another credit and afterward offers the home to you, the merchant's advance must be paid back promptly or face dispossession.

This is because of a legitimate provision composed into almost every advance called the "Due on Sale" condition. This provision gives the previous loan specialist the privilege to call the loan instantly due. On the off chance that that sum can't be paid, the loan specialist has the privilege to abandon the property. A few financial specialists decide to overlook this provision and still buy "subject to" the other credit, taking a chance thinking that the bank won't dispossess.

On the off chance that the conditions are correct, proprietor financing can be an incredible approach to pick up responsibility for bequest without utilizing a bank. Proprietor financing can likewise be a decent instrument for financing your properties later on also.

Direct Money

"Direct cash" is financing that is gotten from private business or individual with the end goal of putting resources into land. While terms and styles change frequently, Hard Money has a few characterizing attributes:

- Loan is essentially in light of the property's estimation

- Less length of terms

- Larger than ordinary interest (6-12%)

- High credit "focuses" (charges to get the advance)

- Many hard cash moneylenders don't oblige salary confirmation

- Many hard cash moneylenders don't oblige credit references

- Does not appear on your own credit report

- Hard cash can regularly subsidize an arrangement in not more than days

- Hard cash loan specialists comprehend when the property needs recovery work

Hard cash can be useful for fleeting advances and circumstances; however numerous financial specialists who have utilized hard cash moneylenders have been put in extreme circumstances when the transient advance ran out. Utilize hard cash with alert, verify that you have different procedures to get and outset them up before taking out a hard cash credit.

To locate a hard cash loan specialist, attempt the accompanying tips:

- Ask a Property Agent

- Ask a Property Flipper

- News

- Search it on the net

- Brokers

Private Money

Private cash is like hard cash in numerous regards, yet is generally recognizable because of the relationship between the bank and the borrower. Regularly, with "private cash," the loan specialist is not an expert moneylender like a hard cash bank, but instead an individual hoping to accomplish higher profits for their money. In many cases, there is a cozy association with a private cash loan specialist, and these moneylenders are substantially less "business" situated than hard cash banks. Furthermore, private cash more often than not has less charges and focuses, and the term length can be arranged all the more effectively to serve the best enthusiasm of both sides.

Private loan specialists will give you tips to purchase property for a particular interest rate. Their venture is secured by a promissory note or home loan on the property that implies on the off chance that you don't pay; they can abandon and take the house (simply like a bank, hard cash, or most other credit sorts). The premium rate given to a private loan specialist is generally settled in advance and the cash is loaned for a predefined timeframe, anywhere in the range of four months to thirty years.

A private loan specialist ordinarily does not get any value stake in income future quality outside of their pre-decided interest rate; however, there are no firm guidelines in terms of private capital. For the most part, one financial specialist finances private cash. These credits are additionally ordinarily utilized when you trust you can raise the property's estimation over a brief timeframe so you can tackle the obligation from that private cash, renegotiate the property in the wake of including esteem, and pay back the private moneylender. Much the same as with hard cash, private cash ought to just be utilized when you have different, plainly characterized exit procedures.

Equity Loans and Credit Lines

Numerous speculators decide to take advantage of the value in their own essential home to help fund the buy of their venture properties. Banks and other giving organizations have a wide range of items that permit you to take advantage of the assets that you currently own. For instance, a speculator may buy a property, however rather than experiencing the ordinary bother of attempting to back the venture property itself, they can rather take out an alone home loan to pay for the property.

So as to acquire a home value advance or line of credit, you should first have value in your home. Banks will commonly just loan up to a sure rate of your home's estimation altogether. This rate varies between loan specialists, yet it is not unprecedented to locate a giving establishment that will offer to give up to 50% of the estimation of your home.

Utilizing home value advances and lines of credit have various advantages over conventional advances, including:

• Loan depends on the estimation of your essential habitation - not the recently bought property. This implies that the bank that is giving the advance won't regularly even take a gander at the new property. They don't for the most part fret about what your expectation is with the cash, just your capacity to pay it back. All things considered, the new property can be in frightful condition, and the bank likely won't give it a second thought.

• When you have a home value credit or line, the cash is yours to do with what you need. It's not subject to the new property - so you can offer "money" when making offers on new properties, and accordingly, you will have a higher possibility of getting your offers acknowledged.

• Home value lines and advances may have certain tax breaks, for example, the capacity to deduct the hobby paid on that credit that is permitted by the law.

• Because the advance is secured by your essential living arrangement, the premium rate on home value advances and lines is regularly low contrasted with hard cash or private cash.

Another method frequently utilized by financial specialists is to utilize a little bit of their home value to subsidize the upfront installment on their venture property.

At long last, home value credits and lines accompany both settled and flexible interest rates. Make sure to take a gander at your objectives, timetables, and budgetary position when figuring out which home value item you need to use to promote your contributing profession.

Association

In the event that you need to put resources into a bit of property, yet the value extent is outside of your wallet, a value accomplice may be an appreciated expansion to your group. A value accomplice is somebody that you get into help you back the property in exchange of giving them a part of the returns. Associations can be organized in a wide range of courses, from utilizing an accomplice's money to back the whole property, to utilizing an accomplice to just reserve the initial installment. There are no set "guidelines" with value associations, yet every circumstance and arrangement obliges its own investigation of how the arrangement will be assembled, who settles on the choices, and how benefits will be parted towards the end.

The value accomplice may have a dynamic or latent part in the property. The possession of a certain part of the property by the value accomplice may permit that accomplice to effectively take part in about all parts of property proprietorship. Moreover, as an accomplice, they commonly get as per their proprietorship rate an arrival on their speculation that incorporates income, thankfulness, deterioration, and consequent benefit when the property is sold.

Not at all like a private moneylender, a value accomplice might not get settled upon a premium rate on their cash. Rather, they get just a small rate of what the property produces. In the event that it profits then, their returns will be higher, yet in the event that the venture loses cash, they may need to contribute cash to keep the property above water. Value accomplices take a higher danger than a private bank may yet consequently, they have the capability of making fundamentally more when the venture is fruitful. Likewise, not at all like in private giving, the value accomplice's speculation is not secured by a home loan or promissory note, but rather by a working regulation between the accomplices.

Loans for Commercial Purposes

While the above alternatives concentrate essentially on the private side of advances, the universe of business loaning may likewise be a feasible choice towards the contribution that you need. Truth be told, in the event that you are hoping to purchase a property other than a two to five unit private property, a business advance is likely precisely what you'll be requiring.

Business advances normally have somewhat higher interest rates and expenses, and in addition shorter terms and distinctive qualifying measures. In the realm of private giving, the borrower's salary is esteemed above each other region; business loaning, then again, is a great deal more centered on the property. The rationale behind this is straightforward: in the event that you claim a two million dollar condo building and things turn out badly, you wouldn't have the capacity to make that home loan installment on the off chance that you make dollar ten thousand every year or dollar hundred thousand every year in individual wages. The business bank will at present take a gander at your salary, credit, and other individual budgetary pointers. In addition, in the dominant part of most cases is the measure of income a property produces.

Chapter 17
Simple Tips to follow

There are many things that you need to take of when you jump into the world of real estate, over the past few years that you might have been in this field you must have noticed how uncertain the market is and how difficult it can be to get great return on your investment without any problems. There are various things that you need to focus upon when you enter the world of real estate, you can't simply think that buying a property is all that it takes. Instead, you have to make sure that you think about what you will do in advance that is you plan about what you are going to do. Planning is the most important aspect of any project and unless and until you make a proper plan that states how you will achieve your desired goals, you won't be able to get where you want to go. Planning can be difficult so try to take help from other people who are more experienced; there are plenty of books on the Internet that can be helpful to your cause. The first step that you should talk when entering the world of real estate is to make sure that you know what you want to achieve. You need to know that real estate is a proper business and not just an extra activity that you can undertake. You have to dedicate a lot of time towards it and at times this can be very difficult. If you have another job that you are doing along with investing in properties, make sure that you have a perfect balance between the two jobs. You can't just quit your job. Imagine the kind of house that you want and picture it in your mind again and again. Even if you are looking to invest or a buy a home for yourself, this is the ideal house that anyone would wish to but because anyone who wishes to make extra money simply wants to have all the comforts that the world has to offer. So, try to make sure that the house that you imagine is a comfortable one that anyone would wish to buy. Don't try to stereotype and invest in only a particular type of house but expand your horizon to include a lot of things. This way you can cater to the needs of a lot of people and everyone would wish to buy your house. The most people that are interested in buying your house the greater the chances are getting a proper return on your investment. When you plan you have to study all the alternative courses of action that you can take and decide from which one you want to pursue. Hence, you have to think about the various steps that you can take in achieving your goals and decide which suits your need. Don't just have an overview of what you want to achieve but rather make sure that everything you decide has many details to it. This guarantees that one way or another you will get success. Why should you even think about investing real estate? The answer is: to have enough cash to live on when we can't work no more or have no wish to work. To set that cash aside, on the other hand, we need to sufficiently collect to counterbalance expansion and the expenses that dissolve our funds. Also, for that reason, land is a phenomenal arrangement.

The colossal thing about land is that even in an awful economy, it will for the most part be superior to anything else. Land, all things considered, is a limited asset. Individuals require a spot to live, work, shop and play - so land is truly simply a question of supply and request.

In addition, land will keep on acknowledging incidental moderate downs in the economy. Truth be told, it's turned out to be the most ideal approach to make riches. Here are a few tips, then, for business people on beginning and succeeding in the property business:

Plan

Before you purchase that first property, or do your first examination, figure out what you anticipate from your speculations. What are your money related objectives? We frequently talk about the "time versus cash" idea: The more you have of one, the less you need of the other to achieve your budgetary objectives. This implies that you shouldn't shy away from setting aside an ideal opportunity to comprehend your objectives and verify every speculation so that you can work towards accomplishing them. On the off chance that you are uncertain precisely how to make money related objectives, meeting with a monetary guide is a magnificent first step.

Control your expenses

You completely need to realize a few simple things before wandering into investing. Along these lines, make certain to do some concentrate homework; however, don't let "purchasing and gathering" data turn into your endgame. Once more, having an objective personality a top priority will make the procedure a great deal more clear. It's anything but difficult to get so tied up in the "exploration" stage that you never really make a move. Rather, record particular inquiries you need addressed or objectives you need to meet before diving into the most recent book/class/and so forth.

Look at many properties

Don't simply snatch the first property you take a gander at. An excess of financial specialists purchase properties on the grounds that they "look decent," or the speculators would prefer not to put the work into take a gander at what's truly out there. Recollect that, you won't be living there so don't settle on your speculation choice in light of your own inclinations. While you shouldn't fall into the trap of examination loss of motion, verify you are careful in looking through properties. Give yourself an extensive variety of choices, and then restricted them down taking into account the criteria (objectives) you have set for yourself.

Don't wait for the right property to just show up

A lot of new financial specialists experience the ill effects of "a-superior arrangement may-be-practically around the bend" disorder. This can blowback in a major manner, and you could conceivably neglect an incredible arrangement simply on the grounds that you're waiting for something better. Your undertaking may feel troublesome if this is your first property, however you must understand that the "ideal arrangement" infrequently exists. Better to execute on an arrangement that meets the greater part of your criteria than sit tight for another that may never come.

Money related expansion

Be practical. Take a detailed look into each and every option before deciding which course of action that you want to pursue. What's more, never purchase property at a higher cost or on less alluring terms than the prices that appeared in your examination. Be careful about dealers that attempt to over-gauge the property's estimation through assessed information. While you can positively utilize a specific/estimated idea to begin the discussion, verify you know the genuine numbers before shutting. Look at earlier years' government forms, property-expense charges, support records, and so forth to get a smart thought of the genuine wage and costs.

The most imperative figures you ought to know are:

- Wages and costs

- Cash stream (net wage/obligation financing installments)

- Return on speculation (income/venture)

- Cap rate (net wage/property cost)

- Cash-on-money return (income/venture)

- Total rate of interests (aggregate return/speculation)

When you have comprehended these figures, you ought to have enough data to figure out if or not procuring the property fits with your monetary.

Be careful when buying the property

On the off chance that the dealer is spurred to offer, you're not prone to get the value best adjusted to your money related objectives. Things being what they are, how would you know whether a merchant is spurred? Look at the asking cost. Obviously, this brings up the issue of how to discover propelled dealers. There are numerous methodologies, and one of these will work for you, contingent upon what property you need. Be that as it may, a couple trusted strategies include:

• Attending open houses

• Looking for empty properties that are available to be purchased

• Spreading the word about yourself and what properties you are searching for - genuinely

• Searching for the antiquated course and looking in the classifieds of your nearby paper

These are only a couple of approaches to discover merchants, however there are conceivably many different strategies, contingent upon what sort of property you're searching for.

Land contributing

As a business visionary, you as of now have a business, and land contributing are best used to bolster that business, not supplant it - unless that is your aim. As it were, don't get so found up in executing exchanges that your center business wavers. On the off chance that that happens, you'll be confronting a rough street to return to dependability. Unless your business is itself property or you're hoping to get into the business full-time, never forget that seeking after these arrangements is an unfortunate obligation, not an end unto itself.

Chapter 18

FAQs on Buying/ Selling Property

When it comes to investing in real estate, it is obvious that you will have a few doubts on the topic. In this chapter, we will look at these questions in detail and answer them to help you understand the topic better.

Are property investments good choices?

Yes. Property investments are great choices. It is important to note that you can increase your investment's worth over a period of time. What you buy today will grow in value over time and you can realize a profit from it. These investments are good for both small and big investors as a plethora of investment options are available. It is a matter of looking for the best options available to you. You can also invest in multiple properties if you wish to diversify your real estate portfolio.

Who can invest?

Anybody interested in buying a property can invest in real estate. A major, i.e. someone above the age of 18 can freely buy and sell property; provided they have the right means to do so. A minor too can buy and sell property, provided a major is assisting them. If you wish to increase your money's worth over a period of time then you can invest in real estate. If you wish to buy a place to call your own and provide your family a place to live in freely without worrying about the rent, then you can buy a property. There is no limit on why you should or should not buy a property of your choice.

How long does it take to own?

That depends on what you are looking to buy. Buying a house can take about a month's time and longer if you are looking for your dream house. It might take a long time for you to buy a commercial property and much longer if you wish to construct it. It will also take a long time for you to buy recreational property. It is best that you keep 6 months as the time limit for buying the ideal property for yourself. But remember that patience is a virtue and there is no point in rushing your home buying process. Never settle for the first place that you see. Keep looking and have at least 2 choices ready before deciding on any one of the houses to buy.

Can I transfer it to someone?

Yes. You can transfer your property to anybody you like. That decision will fully lie with you and you can choose to transfer the property to anybody that you like. It is not necessary that you have children and you transfer the property to them. You can transfer it to any family member that you like. It only takes signing a few property papers and your property will be transferred to them. You can also buy a property in another person's name like your wife or child's name. Although you will be paying for it, the property will belong to the person in whose name you bought it.

Is inherited property an investment?

No. When you inherit a property, you are handed it down and you don't really pay anything towards it. That therefore does not count as your investment. An investment is one where you pay out of your own pocket and buy something. Inherited property can be converted into a lucrative property by renting it out but it will not really count as your investment. If you have paid a certain sum towards the property before owning it despite it being an inherited property then it will count as your investment.

Will I have to pay a lot of taxes?

Not really. When you buy a house, you are exempt from paying certain taxes. But you will have to bear property and other such taxes that the government will levy on you. There is a chance for you to save on this tax by making use of certain techniques. It is important that you remain well versed with all the different taxes that are levied on property in your state.

Is capital gain taxed?

Yes. Capital gain is taxable. Whether you earn a rent or any other form of capital gain, a tax will be levied on it. You have to pay the tax to avoid any problems. This tax is generally a small percentage of your income. Here too, it is possible for you to avoid paying the tax in full. You will be taxed for all gains from your different properties. The tax levied on gain earned from foreign investments is the same as what you will earn from your local properties. So it is important to understand how much tax is levied on capital gains. However, the advantage is that, you can deduct an equivalent amount from the tax that you will pay in your home country. This means that you will not have to pay the same amount in two countries thereby saving on your home country's tax. This very aspect encourages people to invest in foreign properties.

Should I hold on to all my properties?

Not necessarily. You need not hold on to your properties. You can sell them if you wish to and use the money for something else. You can buy and sell your properties as and when you like. If you think you can earn a profit out of it then it is best that you dispose off your property.

What are REITs?

REITs stand for real estate investment trusts. REITs are listed in the stock market and are traded on a daily basis. The money that is collected from it is pooled in and houses or apartments are constructed. You can buy these houses and they are generally priced low. The money that is collected from you is given to the investors in the form of interest on investment.

Is property investment part of my portfolio?

Yes. Property investments are part of your portfolio investments. They will count as your taxable investments and will appear in your portfolio investments. If you have REITs as well, then that will appear separately in your portfolio investment sheet.

Are foreign investments worth it?

Yes. Foreign investments help you diversify your real estate portfolio. You can benefit greatly from your foreign investments. Try to invest in a country where the real estate is booming. You can also invest in multiple countries if you have the budget for it. But remember that you will have to pay taxes for all your investments and it will depend on the countries laws and political stand on foreign investments.

What are REIAS?

REIAS are real estate investors association. These are associations where you can have access to real estate agents, property buyers, sellers, renters, leasers etc. all under the same roof. You can make use of these to find the ideal property for yourself.

These form the different FAQs that are generally asked on the topic and hope you had yours answered efficiently.

Chapter 19

Real Estate Investments Around the World

These countries were all chosen based on a recent survey on the best places to invest your money in the world. They are not listed in any particular order and are mentioned randomly.

Real estate in England

It is a good idea for you to invest in real estate in a foreign country, especially if the country is known for its soaring property prices.

Let us look at 5 criteria that you have to consider when it comes to investing in properties in a foreign country. The where to buy will tell you the best places where you can invest in the country, how to buy refers to the buying procedure that you have to follow, how much you might have to shell out and also the pros and cons of investing in the country.

We will look at 12 different countries that you can consider investing in.

<u>Where to buy</u>

There are many good places in the UK to buy property but London is one of the most preferred places.

It is no secret that London is a beautiful place. You can invest in property there and increase your money's worth.

Right from posh countryside estates to new age homes located in the city, London is one of the most preferred investment hubs for celebrities and several businessmen. Apart from the stable economy of the county, London also provides other investment options.

When it comes to understanding the best locations in a county, it is best to make a list and then narrow it down. Let us now look at the best places in the North of London that will help you increase your money's worth.

Chelsea

Home to one of the wealthiest football clubs in the world; Chelsea is a real estate investor's paradise. Although it does not provide a picturesque view of rivers, Chelsea has an old world charm that is sure to help you settle in well. It is believed that property prices here will increase by 26% in the next 5 years and therefore makes for a great investment choice for you.

Westminster

Probably the most famous name in London, Westminster is a great place to own property. Although the prices will be really high, you can expect a growth of 25.6% within 5 years. That makes it a great investment avenue.

Hackney

For those looking to invest in East London, it does not get any better than Hackney. Home to the 20102 London Olympics, the area saw a rise in property investments and continues to be a preferred location.

Haringey

Haringey is seen as one of the most affluent places to buy property in London. It houses some of the most picturesque locations in the world. Right from Alexandra Park to Muswell hill, the places provides for great real estate locales. It is believed that investing in a property here will help you increase its worth by 20% within 5 years.

Lambeth

Lambeth located in South London is possibly the best place to invest in property in London. Lambeth houses the river on one side, and leafy suburbs on the other! It is estimated that property prices will rise by 21.4% and remain to be one of the most valuable investment avenues in London.

Wandsworth

Wandsworth is known to charge the lowest council tax in the country and possibly the reason why many investors prefer to invest there. The real estate prices are expected to rise by 21.9% in the coming years, which makes the place a great choice for you.

How to buy

When it comes to buying a property in London, you will first have to understand what the trending prices look like. For that, you can go through a building survey that will cost you around 500 Pounds or $700 but will be well worth it, as it will contain the listings of all the best places. Another option is the homebuyer's report, which will cost you around 300 Pounds or $400, and will also contain great information that will help you make your choice. Once you find the property, you will have to get in touch with the owner and your legal team. Once your lawyer or lawyers go through all the details, he or she will suggest the next move. It is best to allow at least 1 year of research and miscellaneous time to find and move to the property.

How much to pay

A regular 2-bedroom apartment of about 175 sq. m. in London might cost you 500,000 Pounds or $733,180. But that might not help you convert it into a great investment. A villa in Westminster might cost 19,950,000 Pounds or $30,253,882 but will help you realize a sizeable profit from it.

Pros

There are many advantages to investing in real estate in London. As you saw, the prices will rise by a large profit margin within a short period of time. Another major advantage of investing in London is that, it is pro landlord! This means that you will have the chance to avail many benefits from letting out your house for rent in London. The landlord will have it easy to set the rent and can also demand a deposit that will cover for the rent for a few months. The taxes are also quite nominal in London and you will not have to worry too much about them. Your team of lawyers will help you pay them and you won't have to do too much towards it. A 150 sq. m. apartment can fetch you around 5,000 Pounds or $8,000 a month.

<u>Cons</u>

The major cons of investing in London are the high prices. As you saw, the prices have sky rocketed in the last few years and it is not as cheap as it once was. You will have to pay a lot of money to begin with and also worry about the taxation.

However, a real estate investment in London will prove to be quite a lucrative choice if you invest in a big villa in a posh location.

Real estate in France

How would it feel to own a house in the French Riviera? Wouldn't it be amazing to have a villa that overlooks the French countryside? Well, all of it sounds quite enticing no doubt but before any of it, you will have to understand the real estate scene in France.

France houses beautiful cities like Paris and Versailles. But since Paris is the most iconic city in France, most people prefer to invest there without exploring some of the better options the country has to offer.

<u>Where to buy</u>

Riviera

The Riviera is where most posh people prefer to invest their money. Les Issambres is a great location for you to pick to own a posh home in France.

Olonzac

Olonzac is a great place in the south of France and is an undervalued area to invest in. The area is close to the coast and quite picturesque. A 4 bedroom flat in the area will cost you about 75,000 Pounds or $110,000 and will make for a great holiday home. You can also give it away to rent and earn a great return on your investment.

Cannes

Famous for the film festival, Cannes is a great place for you to invest your money. You will have the chance to own a property in one of the poshest locations in France. Right from stylish people to yacht owning millionaires, Cannes is home to a wide array of personalities. A house or a villa here is sure to put you on the real estate radar.

The Tran

If you wish to own a property that is away from the hustle and bustle and houses quiet and calm surroundings, then the Tran is a great option for you. It is a picturesque countryside that is unexplored. You will have the chance to invest in a house and might also get a land big enough to do some gardening/ farming.

French Alps

If you are thinking of going all out and investing in a posh locality where there is not a single vehicle to pollute the air and surrounded by lush green mountains, then the French Alps are the place to be. Not only will you have the chance to explore the surroundings on a bike but will love the winter months when skiing will be your favorite sport.

Mont Saint Michel

If you are interested in an area that is mostly frequented by tourists owing to the presence of some of the best castles in France, then Mont Saint Michel in Normandy is the place to be. The property prices here are said to rise consistently owing to the posh locales. A cottage here would equate to a great property investment for you.

Paris

Paris houses some of the most famous landmarks in the world. One amongst them is the Eiffel tower. But it is highly unlikely that you will be able to build a home under it and will have to settle for other places in the city. The prices can be a bit high if you pick villas but 2 bedroom flats will be charged nominally. You can also fetch a great rent if you buy the property near some of the fashion markets in Paris.

How to buy

In order to buy a property in France, you have to go through a directory. There you will find the names and contacts of the owners and also a few pictures of the properties. Once you decide on it, you will have to contact the owner and also you lawyer. Thanks to the internet, you will have it much more easily as you can look at the different property pictures online. You will have to pay 7.5% of the purchase price as commission towards your real estate purchases in France. It is best to be informed about the different little details before going ahead with the investment. You will also have to employ an analyst who will value your property for you.

How much to pay

Although France is a great place to invest in given the rich natural locales and amazing views, the property prices are not that high. This very aspect makes France a great place to invest your money. A villa in Cannes might cost you around 500,000 euro or 345,000 Pounds or $500,000. A house in mount saint Michel will cost you 263,000 euros. You will have to reason out with the owner and arrive at a price that you think matches the property. 430,000 euros should be your ideal budget if you wish to own a property by the Riviera. You might have to shell out a bit more if you wish to buy a property in Paris and have a budget of 700,000 euros.

Pros

As you know, France is one of the most visited places in Europe. You will have the chance to live in a place that is both picturesque and connects well to the rest of Europe. The laws of the land are also in favor of the owners and investors will have it easy when they wish to invest in France.

Cons

There are a few cons that come your way when you wish to invest in France. The first con is the pro tenant laws of the land. This means that the country's laws favor the tenant and give them more privilege. Another disadvantage is that most people prefer to own a holiday home in France and that might make it a bit difficult for you to find a consistent tenant. The value of real estate properties in France is said to have gone down in the last few years.

Real estate in Spain

Spain is the next most visited country in Europe after France and owning a property here will help you increase your money's worth.

Spain is viewed as an underdog in the property market. The continuous evolving economic norms in the country is said to make Spain a hotspot for real estate investments.

<u>Where to buy</u>

Catalonia

Catalonia is a great little region in Northern Spain. It is full of beaches and picturesque locales. As per a recent survey, Catalonia is the most preferred region in Spain to make real estate investments. Many call it a hub to earn passive income, as there is a lot of demand for real estate in Catalonia. You are sure to find fully functional homes that have the best views from all the rooms.

Canary Islands

The second most preferred place in Spain to make real estate investments is the Canary Islands. Although regarded as one of the most far-flung areas of the country, the Canary Islands are viewed as one of the best areas to invest in Spain. It is covered in many beaches that are moistly flanked by short picturesque hills. There is also the world famous national park along with an observatory. Canary Islands are home to many celebrity homes and buying a property here is sure to help you get noticed by some of the big wigs in the world of real estate.

Andalucía

Andalucía is located in the southern most region of Spain and is known for its sun kissed hills. Home to most tourist attractions in Spain including flamenco dancers and bull fighters, Andalucía is a great place to make real estate investments. There is a lot to do in the region and an investment there will help you convert your investment into riches. Seville is particular is where it would be best for you to look for the ideal property. The University of Granada is also located close by and is quite popular. If you are keen on having a home that is located in a natural setting away from populated cities then Andalucía is the place for you.

Balearic Islands

The Balearic Islands are a must visit in Spain and also a great property investment site. Located off the eastern coast of Spain, the Balearic Islands are beautiful and full of white sandy beaches. It is an archipelago and contains several islands. Mallorca is the biggest and the most prolific of islands and is where many famous people find their homes.

Madrid

The capital city of Spain, Madrid has some great properties on offer to homebuyers. Madrid enjoys great climate all year long and is full of beautiful castles that are strewn all over the city. Real estate in Madrid is said to have boomed in the last few years and continues to escalate as the economy of Spain has bettered considerably.

How to buy

To start with, you will have to go through the listed properties in the area of your choice. Once you find the ideal location and the best house, you have to get in touch with your lawyer. Remember that it is also a great option for you to pick a local lawyer in Spain who will be able to help you a lot better. Funding of the property can be done through a local bank like the bank of Spain, which will assist you with the property buying.

How much to pay

The real estate prices in Spain will differ from region to region. A place in Catalonia will cost you around 192,000 euros or 140,000 Pounds or $200,000. It is also the most expensive place in Spain. A house in the Canary Islands will cost you around 200,000 euros or 145,000 Pounds or $210,000. A house in Andalucía will cost you around 143,000 Pounds and one in the Balearic islands will be around 215,000 Pounds or $310,868. All of these will make for great investments provided you pick the best locations.

Pros

The recent land laws have all made owning a property in Spain a great choice for both budding investors and old hands. You will have the chance to own a property in a great country that has a lot to see and do. You can buy a property and convert it into a holiday home if you like. It is also quite close to the rest of the European countries and its prime location is one of the major attractions of Spain. An apartment in Spain can help you earn between 3,500 to 5,000 euros a month depending on its location. That is sure to help you make up for your investment within a short time.

Cons

The high taxes in Spain are a cause of concern for many. They view it as a drawback for those wanting to invest in real estate. In fact, Spain has one of the highest property taxes that are levied on estates in the whole of Europe. Apart from that, the laws of the land are pro tenant. So, your tenant will enjoy better privileges when you wish to rent out your place in Spain. That can be a big drawback for those looking to exercise more control over their property. You should also know that you might not easily get property near the coast as most of them are reserved for the locals. So, you might have to settle for something that is located a little away from the coast.

Spain is a great little country in Europe and a property here will be surely worth every penny.

Real estate in Switzerland

Switzerland is generally associated with five star resorts camped in snow-capped mountains and skiing enthusiasts. But what many don't realize is that Switzerland is a great place in Europe to invest your money.

Where to buy

Berne

Berne, the capital of Switzerland is one of the best places to invest in. Berne is located between plateaus in the western region and mountains in the eastern region. This makes the city great for real estate investments. It is the least populated city in Switzerland yet one of the biggest cities in Switzerland. That makes it quite a great place where there will be enough and more space for you. Another aspect about Berne that makes it a great is the shopping promenade that is one of the biggest in Europe.

Zurich

You will not have second thoughts about buying a house in Zurich! The city was rated second in terms of best standard of living in the world and that is enough to tell you how great a place it really is. Zurich is home to some of the best colleges, hospitals and also transportation facilities, all of which make Zurich a great place to live in. The city of Zurich is divided into 12 different districts and each one has a capital. That makes life quite easy. There is a lot on offer in the city in terms of real estate properties.

Basel

Located on the northwestern border of Switzerland, Basel is a great place to buy property as it is bordered by France and Germany. Basel is considered as the cultural center of Switzerland and is great for those looking to invest in a happening place in the country. It is full of shopping centers, restaurants, museums and other such tourist attractions. The transport system in Basel is said to be great as it is flanked by two other major economic destinations in Europe.

Geneva

Geneva is famous for being host to some of the most prolific world organizations such as Red Cross. Geneva is a cultural hub and one of the most visited cities in Switzerland. The transport system and the standard of living in Geneva are great, comparatively better than in Zurich. The standard of living in Geneva is also much higher, making it a place for posh celebrities, sportsmen and politicians. Many trains that carry people to ski resorts pass by this city thereby causing many footfalls a day in the city of Geneva.

Lugano

Located in the southern most region of Switzerland, Lugano is a great little town for you to invest in Switzerland. Lugano is a place where many Italians have settled and makes it seem like little Italy. Right from the cuisine to the architecture, there is a great Italian influence in Lugano, which makes it an interesting confluent place to invest. The prices here are slightly more affordable yet do not compromise on the value of your investments.

How to buy

First and foremost, you must understand that properties are all managed by the Swiss government and governed under the Swiss Federal law. But non-residents will be able to buy properties with ease. However, it is not possible for a nonresident to buy a property in certain parts of Switzerland, mainly in the Northern regions. In fact, the 1440 regions that are available for non-residents to buy from are clearly mentioned. You will have to look up listings in the paper or on the Internet to find the ideal property. Once you do, you have to contact the owner and agree on a price. You can then get your lawyer involved in it. You have to understand that you will need lesser permission to make it your main home where you will reside and more if you plan on renting or leasing it out. You will have to make it clear as to what you wish to do with your property.

How much to pay

The property prices in Switzerland vary from place to place. It depends on the area and also the surroundings. You can avail a loan from a local bank and buy the property. A house in Zurich might cost you 500,000 Pounds or $733,180. A home in Basel might cost you around 300,000 Pounds or $440,000. Most houses you get will be fully furnished and come with décor. But you have the freedom to change it up as per your choice. Most buyers will only accept Swiss francs from you, which is the local currency in Switzerland. Swiss francs are one of the strongest currencies in the world and so; you might have to exchange a lot of your local currency to attain them. You have to plan everything out well in advance.

<u>Pros</u>

Switzerland is flanked by Germany, France, Italy and Austria. Its prime location, right in the center of Europe makes it a great place to settle down. Even if you will not be able to earn a lot by letting out apartments, you will still have the chance to earn quite a bit by letting out holiday homes. A home let out in Zurich might fetch you 11,000 euros a month, which is quite good considering the initial investment that you would have made to acquire the land. But this amount will differ based on the size of the property and also its location.

<u>Cons</u>

There are some cons to investing in Switzerland. One problem you will face is the weather. It is mostly cold in Switzerland and the snow can block roads quite often. Travelling in an out of Switzerland to buy/ sell/ rent property might get a bit tricky. The real estate industry was also hit in the last decade as more and more investors preferred to put their money in Spanish estates. Another major problem in Switzerland that might deter investors is the high rate of income tax that needs to be paid. You might have to pay quite a bit of money towards tax on the rental income that you earn from your property investment, which might eat away into your profits.

Real estate in Singapore

Apart from European countries, there are also some Asian countries that are great places to invest with in real estate. One such great Asian country is Singapore. Singapore is regarded as the best place to live in the world and rightly so.

Many people get confused wondering as to what Singapore really is. Well, Singapore is an island city off the southern coast of Malaysia. Some consider it a country while some others refer to it as a city-state.

Where to buy

Orchard road

Orchard road is a great road in Singapore to buy property. It is located in the heart of the city and is well connected to the rest of the places. There are many restaurants, spas, schools and colleges located here. A house here will help you command a great rent. Several expats have also settled here making it one of the best places in Singapore to buy property and also settle down.

Holland village

Holland village is another great location for you. It is a convenient spot and has many expats who have settled there. The place is full of nice restaurants and is close to the center.

Holland village is also close to the Botanic gardens, which makes for a nice place to escape to. Holland village is quite serene and sure to help you settle in easily.

Sentosa

Sentosa is possibly the best area in Singapore to buy a house. Sentosa is a great little area located in the heart of Singapore. The houses are all mostly located right on the sea that makes it a great location for the elite to settle. There is easy access to the motorways and you will find it rather easy to access the different restaurants, malls and also spas. The prices here might be quite high but you can easily make up for it by renting it out to expats and others that settle in the area.

Upper Bukit Timah

If you are interested in having a property in the middle of a forest then you can look up houses in upper Bukit Timah. The area is a great place for nature lovers and is quite close to Orchard road. You can make use of the different amenities that are on offer and will help you connect to the rail with ease. Here too, the prices can be a bit high but will be easy for you to make up for it by giving the house away to expats that wish to stay there.

How to buy

There is a standard procedure that you will have to follow if you are a resident of USA to buy a house in Singapore. To start with, you have to contact an agent in Singapore who will help you find the right house. In all these instances, it is best for you to have a local friend who will assist you. Then, you should hunt for the house. Once you find it, you will have to meet the owner and also take your lawyer or solicitor along. Once everything is settled, you can get keys to the apartment or condo. You will have to check if it is possible for you to start renting the place out with immediate effect. If so, you can begin looking for your tenant. Some people prefer to stay in the house for a little while and then rent it out. You too can do the same.

How much to pay

Singapore is priced high. There are many villas, apartments and condos there and each one is priced quite high. You will have to set a realistic budget if you wish to buy a house there. A condo in the heart of Singapore might cost you $500,000. You will have to check the trending prices to be sure and also might have to go through the latest price journals.

Pros

Singapore is a great place to live. It is the one place in Asia which is said to be safe in terms of economy and more and more people are planning on settling down there. The government here is said to be one of the best in the world. When you buy a house, condo or villa in Singapore, you will not have to pay a hefty transaction cost. It is quite nominal and something that will not break your bank. It is in fact the lowest amongst the Asian countries in terms of value of the property. The tax system in Singapore is also great. There is no tax on income up till $15,000. A 2 bedroom flat in Orchard road will help you earn around $10,000 a month. You will have to look for one that is located in the heart of the city and comes with modern amenities.

Cons

Since Singapore is a popular destination for many big celebrities and businessmen, the prices quoted by homeowners are quite high. Most condos will cost you around $15,000 per sq. m. and a 500 sq. m. condo will cost you $7500000. That is seen as being a bit too much by most investors and will require them to be prepared with a large amount. Another con is that people will have to find the right agent in order to land the best jobs. There will be a plethora of agents to choose from and it will be quite important for you to look for a reliable one. You can go through a list of agents and pick the one with the highest rating.

Real estate in Japan

Apart from Singapore, Japan is a great place in Asia to invest. Better known as the pearl of the orient, Japan is a developed country. The land of japan is split into 4 different parts namely Hokkaido, Honshu, Shikoku and Kyushu. There are about 6850 islands in Japan. All of these are separated by a small straight that runs in between them.

Japan is home to a lot of technological advancements and known as a market for several businesses. No wonder many expats from all over the world prefer to settle there.

<u>Where to buy</u>

Tokyo

Tokyo is the capital of Japan and a great place for you to invest your money. Many investors are interested in Tokyo owing to the upcoming Olympics in 2020. Generally, such events cause the realty prices to rise in value and so; you can capitalize on the same. Tokyo is a very convenient to live in and has great transport systems in place. Its new and upcoming infrastructure is said to be state of the art world class and has already won many awards. Tokyo is slightly more expensive compared to the other parts of japan but that is only acceptable given it is the capital of the country.

Kyoto

Kyoto was once the capital of japan and had a flourishing industry. Kyoto is full of temples and makes it the religious capital of japan. On the other end, many Geishas entertain guests in the various teahouses located all over Japan. But despite maintaining its old world charm, Kyoto has many modern amenities such as posh restaurants and also spas and other such. This makes Kyoto an ideal location to pick. In fact, many people consider Kyoto as the cultural hub of japan and prefer to invest there instead of Tokyo.

Fukuoka

Fukuoka is the capital of Kyushu and one of the best places in japan to invest in real estate. It is also one of the most crowded owing to its proximity to the mainland. The land is flanked by natural monuments such as hills on three sides and a bay on the fourth. Having such a surrounding makes Fukuoka a great place for people to invest in real estate. That's not all, there are many civilian recreational amenities present such as biking parks and boutiques that will help people settle in with ease. In 2006, the city was named as one of the 10 most dynamic cities to live in the world and ever since has seen a radical change in the demand for properties. A 2014 survey stated that Fukuoka is a very livable city and voted best city to settle in the coming years.

Sapporo

If you wish to invest in an area that is away from the tropical climate and more towards a wintery snowcapped location then Sapporo is the one for you. Sapporo is located on the northern most region of Japan in Hokkaido. It snows here most of the year and the ski resorts are quite the tourist destination. Apart from snowcapped hills, there are also many other tourist attractions such as museums, shopping malls etc. It snows the most in the month of April or May and is a great time for you to visit the place and buy a property.

Yokohama

Japan's second largest city, Yokohama is a great place for you to buy property. It is known for its cultural exposure and also different spas, malls and other such amenities. Yokohama is a great place to buy an apartment and rent it out.

How to buy

Unlike most other countries in the world, foreigners will find it rather easy to invest. You will not have to know too many things about the country to buy a house there. All you have to do is get in touch with your solicitor and find the right house. From there, you will have to pretty much follow the same general steps while buying a house.

How much to pay

Homes in Japan have unique structures. Most of them are built to withstand earthquakes and also mostly have cascading roofs. A house in Tokyo might cost you $300,000. You might find it easier to rent out your home in Tokyo as opposed to in any other place in Japan. A place in Kyoto might cost you $500,000. A condo is Sapporo will cost you around $400,000. The population in Sapporo has considerably increased in the last few years and you might have to make do with a cramped space. However, if you don't plan on occupying he place then it is a good location for you to consider in Japan.

Pros

One of the biggest advantages of investing in Japan is the lack of absolutely any restrictions. It is a very liberal country and you don't have to go through a lot to find a place in Japan. You will also find it rather easy to finance your venture in Japan. The banks there will not expect too much in terms of proof from you and will grant it. However, you have to have proof of residence there in order to avail the loan. You will find it rather easy to register your address to a foreign location and have the amount sanctioned within a short period of time. You will benefit as a landlord in Japan. The laws of the land are pro landlords since the year 2000 until when tenants enjoyed more benefits. Rents are generally freely negotiated and arrived at a mutual consensus. The laws also gave landlords more authority to evict the tenants should they overstay in the houses.

Cons

Owning a property in Japan will not entitle you to occupancy. Unless you have a job in Japan and work permit, you cannot occupy your house. But, it will be quite easy for you to rent it out. You will also have to consider the taxes. They are not so low in Japan owing to the constantly improving living conditions. You also might have to pay quite a bit of property tax.

Real estate in Middle East

The Middle East has some of the richest countries in the world. Right from Qatar, which has the highest GDP in the world to Dubai, considered the country of gold. All these countries have great properties on offer and you will surely find it quite easy to settle in.

Where to buy

Qatar

Qatar is a great little country in the Middle East to invest money. Qatar is a developed country and you will find it quite easy to settle in. Doha, the capital city is a great place for you to pick.

The economy is great and so is the landscape, buildings etc. The transport facility here is also great!

Dubai

Dubai is the number 1 destination in the Middle East to make property investments. Dubai has many places that are quite posh and practical to own a house. The several oil fields in Dubai help stabilize its economy and make it the wealthiest country in the Middle East. The best areas in Dubai include palm islands, Dubai marina and the places around the Burj Khalifa. All these places are easily accessible and you will find them great to settle. Another aspect of Dubai is the launch schemes that it has on offer to homebuyers. Buying something when the apartments are just about coming up will help you avail them at discounted prices or get a good deal.

Kuwait

The third and possibly best place in the Middle East is Kuwait. It is close to Qatar and is also quite developed. Kuwait's economy has been extremely steady since a very long time mainly owing to the presence of several financial institutions. Many foreign expats have also made Kuwait their home and are now leading an amazing life owing to their decision. It is believed that Kuwait has the potential of overtaking Dubai's popularity in the near future.

How to buy

One drawback of investing in the Middle East is the excess rules and regulations that are levied. Even though you might find it easy as an expat to buy a house in Dubai or Qatar, you might have to go through a lengthy procedure first. It is also important to find the right agent that will help you find the right home.

How much to pay

A villa in Dubai might cost you around 320,000 Dirhams or $800,000 and one in Qatar might cost you QAR 400,000 or $100,000. It depends on the location and also the amenities that surround the spot.

Pros

A lot of expats have been buying houses in the Middle East off late thereby boosting the real estate business. The rent rates have been surging for quite some time and remain pretty high. You will be surprised at the rate at which the prices have been increasing in Dubai. They are said to further rise, thereby making real estate investments in Dubai a great investment avenue. You will be able to invest now and reap its benefits for several years to come. Qatar is also not too far behind and you will surely avail a great consistent income from your investment for a long time. You will be able to avail around 120,000

Dirhams or $32,000 a month from renting an apartment in central Dubai. It might increase as the area of the house increases and also depends on the area. The transaction cost in Qatar is also quite less. So, you will not have to worry about extra costs getting added on to your final payment.

Cons

There are some cons to investing in the Middle East. One of the biggest con s is the dry arid and excessively hot weather. Many expats find it rather unbearable to settle there, owing to the excess heat. Although most buildings have an air conditioner, it is not easy to settle in with such hot weather. However, buying and renting it out to a local might work in your favor. The taxes that are levied on income earned from property might also be on the higher side. You have to look into how much is being demanded and see whether it is deductible from your tax back in your home country.

Real estate in Australia

In a recent survey conducted on the best cities to live in the world, 5 of the ten belonged to cities in Australia! That's how great the place really is. Here are some tips for homebuyers on where to look for the best houses in Australia.

Where to buy

Australia is a small country and you will have to decide between a few great cities to invest in. here they are.

Melbourne

Melbourne has been voted as the most livable city in the world. It is a great little place to live at and will surely help you adjust well. The city is a delight with many tree-lined streets and Victorian style buildings. It will transport you to a whole new world. There are the royal botanic gardens, which are quite famous and also the national gallery of Victoria. Many upscale apartments and houses are present here and you are sure to find a great place for yourself here. The cricket club here is also quite famous.

Sydney

Sydney, the capital city of South Wales, is a great city to find you home. It houses two of Australia's most iconic monuments namely, the Sydney Opera House and Bondi beach. Sydney has posh houses located by the sea and you will find it rather easy to find a house by the ocean. The prices are highest in Sydney owing to its location and the high demand for properties.

Adelaide

Better known as the cosmopolitan capital of Australia or the soul of south- Australia, Adelaide is a great place to settle down. Known for its art galleries and universities, Adelaide is a great little place for families with children to settle in. the prices for properties in Adelaide have been on a steady rise owing to the demand that has cropped up in the last few years.

Perth

Perth is a great place to settle given its amazing climate. Home to swan valley and a huge aquarium, Perth is one of the most visited cities in Australia. The property prices in Perth are much lower and you will not have to spend too much to avail a house there.

Gold coast

Gold coast is home to several celebrities, sportsmen and other such rich personnel of Australia. Houses there are quite posh and sure to put you amongst the elite. Gold coast is one of the best locations and is full of upscale restaurants, beach resorts etc. Being close to the coast, it is quite warm and comfortable weather wise and what attracts many people to settle. The prices here generally compete with Sydney's prices and you might have to spend quite a bit to find yourself a nice little place.

How to buy

You will first have to get in touch with a local agent who will help you find the right house. Once done, you will have to travel down to Australia. There, you can look at the different places on offer and decide on one. Your lawyer will then get involved and evaluate the property for you. Once done, you can raise the finance through a local Australian bank or through a branch of your local bank. You can then make the payment and get keys to the house. You can occupy it, given you have the permit, or rent it out.

How much to pay

Australia's real estate industry is now booming. Many expats have decided to settle there and also locals are returning back to their homes. There is a lot of demand for houses that causes their prices to rise considerably. This upward increase has caused property prices to surge in the last decade. A 3 bedroom apartment in Sydney will cost you around $2 million whereas a 1 bedroom will cost you around $500,000. An apartment located in gold coast might cost you $400,000.

Pros

The laws in the land are pro landlord this is great as you will have the chance to exercise greater rights over the property. Another advantage is the low transaction costs. You need not shell out a large sum of money towards acquiring a property in Australia and the amount will be quite reasonable. In fact, the stamp duty and legal fees are the lowest in all of the pacific countries and so; you will find it cost effective to invest in Australia. You will have the chance to make around $3000 a month from your 2-bedroom apartment located in Sydney. The price will increase based on the area of the house and also its location.

Cons

The taxes charged in Australia are quite high! Of all the different Asian and pacific countries, Australia will charge you the highest taxes. This is seen as a drawback and most people will think twice. Even if you will be given the chance to deduct it from what you pay in your home country, it will still end up being quite an expensive affair. Therefore, it is best that you know how much you will be taxed before you go about buying a house in Australia.

Apart from these, you can also consider China, Brazil etc. They are also great choices for you.

Andy Anderson

Chapter 20
Things To Consider

• It is extremely important for you to be aware of the exchange rates of the countries. You have to know how much your currency will convert to and what will you be paying towards the house. If you don't have an idea as to the rates of exchange then it is best that you subscribe to a regular journal that will give you all the latest rates. Based on it, you will have the chance to know how much the owner of the house is quoting and whether it is within your budget. Don't ever take a rough statistic and ensure that you know the exact exchange rate. You might have to sit down and calculate a lot and so, it is best to assign an entire day for it.

• You have to get in touch with the best agents in the foreign country. There can be many types of agents and you have to know to spot the best. You can look up their testimonials online to see if they are good for you. If you have a local friend, then you can get them to find out about it for you.

• You can easily reduce your local US tax by deducting the rental income tax that you pay in the foreign country. All you have to do is attach the foreign tax documents and avail the relief.

• It is ideal for you to hold your house for at least 2 to 5 years or longer in order to avail benefits. You will have the chance to avail tax benefits for the period you hold and also during the sale of the property. Availing such dual benefits will further motivate you to hold on to the property and not feel like disposing it off early.

• It is possible for you to buy houses in many countries, provided you plan everything out correctly. You will have to calculate the expenses and also the gains from each of your investments.

Chapter 21
Fixing Credit Score

When it comes to making investments, it is obvious that you will require finance for it. Without finance, you cannot buy a property and that is a no-brainer. But it goes much beyond having enough money or applying for a loan. You have to first know how the credit system works and how you can use it in your favor. It is obvious that the credit system will create troubles if you have a bad score. Before we look at how you can fix your score. We must first look at what the scoring system is all about.

What is it?

As you know, all Americans will be dealt with a credit score to assess their credit worthiness. Credit worthiness refers to being worthy of acquiring credit. This credit refers to the money that you borrow to pay for your different big-ticket items. Some will buy appliances with it, some electronic goods, some cars and some houses. Of these, the last one will be most expensive and will require the person to be quite credit worthy. For that, the person will first have to check their credit report. Credit report refers to the report that carries details of the person's credit worthiness. It contains information about the credit score that the person has earned. Based on what the report contains, the person will be given the loan.

Who will give report?

You can approach any one of the three main credit agencies to help you with your credit report; these include Equifax, Experian or Transunion. These institutions better known, as credit bureaus will lend you the loan based on the credit score that you have. You can apply for your credit report and wait for the union to prepare and share it with you. Once you get your report, you can go through it to see whether it is good or bad.

Why should it be good?

It is important for your credit score to be good. There are many reasons for it like availing loans with ease, getting the loan at a low rate of interest etc. you will feel much confident when you get a good score and will be able to do more financially. In the next segment, we will look at the scoring system and why you should have a good score to begin with.

What are good scores?

<u>Above 700</u>

Getting a score above 700 is great for you! It means that you are extremely credit worthy and can avail a loan for your house with ease. You can also get a great rate of interest, which will be quite less. The bank will not trouble you and will approve your loan within no time. Generally, a score like this is hard to come by unless you have a squeaky-clean track record of paying the borrowed sum on time. Even a single delay in payments can impact your credit score negatively.

<u>680 to 700</u>

680 to 700 is a good score if not a great one. It is what most people will end up getting. Here too, like in the previous category, you will get a good rate of interest that might be slightly lesser as compared to what people in the previous category will get. But it is realistic for you to work with this type of score as compared to the previous one as that can be slightly rare.

<u>620-680</u>

This is an average score. It is not great or bad. It lies in between the two. You will have the chance to avail a loan but not at the interest rate of your choice. It will definitely be higher than what people in the previous range will avail it at.

<u>580-620</u>

This range is quite bad. You will find it difficult to get a loan and the rate of interest will be quite high. Being here will cause people to correct their score at the earliest.

<u>500 -580</u>

This is extremely bad. You will find it really tough to find a loan lender. They will also ask you for a very high rate of interest for it, which might end up being much higher than the borrowed sum itself!

<u>Less than 500</u>

This is the worst and the bottom most range. Being here will surely mean that you will not get a loan and even if you do, the interest will be so ridiculously quoted that you will walk away from it.

What might be some issues in it?

There can be many issues that will contribute towards a bad credit score. First and foremost, check if they have given you the right report and the name is clear and correct. If there is an issue there, then mark it. Next, you should check if the different entries made are all correct. Some creditors might end up mentioning the wrong date of payment of dues that will make it look like you paid late. Another issue might be an erroneous entry. Something that you never borrowed has been mentioned and is being shown as an unpaid expense. You also might spot bills that have been paid late thereby causing a bad credit. You can mark these and have them rectified. You will have to approach the same union again to help fix the errors. They might not be too interested in correcting it unless you force them to. If they are not showing any interest in fixing the errors then you should consider threatening them by saying that you will sue them.

Andy Anderson

Chapter 22

Costs to Calculate while Investing

There are many costs that you should account for when it comes to investing in real estate. You have to be prepared to undertake the different costs involved and pay them on time if you wish to get the house on time. Here is looking at the different fees that you should be aware of and calculate correctly in order to spend the right amount.

Mortgage fees

When it comes to mortgage fees, there are many amounts that you should pay. We will look at them in this segment.

The first amount you will pay is known as the booking fees. This is paid to book the loan amount that you will be acquiring as finance for your real estate investment.

The next fee is known as the arrangement fee. This is paid upfront to the person who is arranging your loan amount. You have to pay them a certain amount for having helped you acquire the loan.

The third fee is generally paid during the end of the mortgage period. It is known as the exit fee and is paid while closing the mortgage account.

Agent's fees

Next, you will have to pay the agent's fees. The agent is someone that will help you find the right property. The agent's fees will be based on how long they have been looking for the house and also the basic value of the house. Generally, a small percentage of it is paid as the agent's fee. The percentage will depend on what has already been agreed upon.

Valuation fees

The next fees are the valuation fees. As you know, your property will have to be assessed by someone who has proper knowledge about properties. He or she will visit your property and check whether it is of good value. They will also give their report on the same. You will have to pay them for their services. It is hard to say how much you might have to pay as it differs from evaluator to evaluator. Some might charge you less and some more based on the type of report that they have prepared for you. If you have sought the advice of a financial advice to avail the loan then you will have to pay them as well. That will also depend on the service provided and the rate of interest that they provided for the loan.

Stamp duty

When you buy a house, you will have to get it registered. It should be registered with a registrar in order to have proof that you have bought the house legally from the owner. For that, you will have to pay a certain stamp duty. The duty is levied based on the amount you have pay towards acquiring the house. It generally differs from country to country. There is no one percentage that is affixed.

Lawyer's fees

You will obviously pay your lawyer for his or her services. It is better known as the Attorney's fees. Generally, a flat rate is agreed upon that the lawyer will intimate before taking up the case. You will have to pay an amount that is agreed upon or whatever the lawyer demands. It is always better to know what the lawyer might demand and be prepared for it. In some cases, the lawyer will demand the fees based on the amount that was paid towards acquiring the house.

Moving expenses

Andy Anderson

If you plan on moving into the new house, then you will surely have to deal with moving expenses. Unless you plan on doing all the packing and moving yourself, you will have to look for packers and movers that will assist you. These packers and movers are generally professionals that know to pack and move belongings professionally. How much they will charge you will completely depend on how much is there to pack and move. If you think they are charging too much and you can pack the stuff yourself then you can simply hire them to move for you. If you wish to further cut down on the expense then you can hire a moving truck, load the stuff yourself and then transport all of it to the new house, the choice if fully yours to make.

Renovation expenses

It is obvious that your new house will not be perfect for you to move in. you will have to renovate it to make it a bit more livable. You will have to first come up with a plan and then see how much it will cost you. You might have to contact a contractor for the job and it will pay to do your homework. You might have to find someone that will give you a good rate for the renovations. You can also check online to find the best contractor by going through the reviews that have been left behind for them.

Fixtures and furniture

Fixing just the walls and roof of the house will not help you move in. You will also have to work on its internal features such as the fixtures and the furniture. You have to factor in the expenses that you will incur when you fix the fans and lights in the house as also the pipes and other such fixtures. You will also have to buy appropriate furniture for the house in order to make it livable. It is always best to have a plan before going about the changes. Remember that some renovation made to the house will help you save on tax and you will have to know what these are. The renovations should be substantial and things that will change the living conditions inside the house.

Amenities

You will also have to provide the tenants with certain amenities such as parking space or swimming pool, gym area etc. These will further cost you and you will have to be prepared to undertake the expenses. Again, you might have the chance to deduct the expenses accrued from the tax that you will be paying.

These are just some of the important fees and are not limited to just these. You should leave a little space for the other costs as well.

Andy Anderson

Chapter 23
Forms of Financing

When it comes to financing both your local property and your foreign property, there are a few standard institutions that you can approach or come up with the money yourself. In this chapter, we will look at some of these in detail.

Personal Savings

Sometimes, the option to turn to is personal savings. This refers to money that you have saved up for yourself and are determined to pump into your real estate investments. Many people set aside a separate account and then use the money for their real estate. You too can do the same. But first you must plan it out correctly and know how much to add to it.

Families

Another option is for you to reach out to family members and ask them for help. They will be able to better guide you and might also provide you with the requisite money to invest. The family member can be someone that has relevant experience in real estate investments and will know to guide you. If they loan out the sum to you then it will be easy for you to pay them back and they might not charge you an interest that is as high as what commercial banks would ask of you.

P2p

There is another great way to raise money for your dream project and it is known as peer-to-peer lending. As you know, peer refers to friend. You can ask your friends to help you out and give you the money. Again, they might give you at a lower interest. However, they might not be able to give you as much money for your investment as a bank would. It might be a bit too farfetched for you to expect them to pay you a large sum. So, you might have to make another arrangement and then combine the two sums.

Credit union

Credit unions are institutions that will help you raise money. They are co-operative societies that set up a financial wing. There, the individual members contribute a certain sum towards it and all of it is pooled together to put in a fund. They will lend the sum to you provided you are a member there. The rate of interest will be quite low as well. However, if you are not a member, then you might find it tough to get the loan. You will need to identify someone who is a member there and ask them to help you out. You can request them to give you the loan if you don't know anyone.

Companies

There can also be some financial companies that will lend you the loan. These companies will be on the lookout for people needing financial aid and will sanction the loan amount. They might charge a large interest though and you have to prepare to pay it. They might also ask you for some collateral that you will have to give to avail the loan.

Foreign investors

You will find many foreign investors interested in giving away loans. These investors will be looking for local country borrowers and will lend it to you if you ask them for the money. The rate of interest offered by them might be much less as compared to what banks will offer you. You don't have to go after foreign investors alone and can also approach locals.

Government schemes

You can also look up to see if there are any governments schemes that you can make use of to avail the loans. Some governments offer schemes to help budding investors. They might have subsidized offers that will help you avail the sum at a discount.

Insurance

It is also possible for you to borrow some money from your insurance company. The company will lend it to you provided you pay the money back on time along with a certain rate of interest.

These form the different ways in which you can raise finance for your real estate investments but is not limited to these. You can exploit other options as well to fund your project.

Taking care of your inherited property

When you inherit property, you will have to take care of it in order for it to remain with you. It is especially important if you have been appointed as the custodian of the property. Here are some things that you will have to do for it.

To start with, you have to appoint someone to look at all the property you hold and give a clear picture of all that is under you. This can include both land and house, and other such immovable properties. Once they find out, you should get them to submit the report to you.

Once done, you should decide on how you wish to divide the property. It depends on who is to benefit from it. Many times, a responsible sibling will be given the job of dividing the property amongst his siblings. If you happen to be one such, then you should plan it out carefully.

You should then get your lawyer involved. Remember that it is always a good idea to go about something legally as opposed to going about it through word of mouth. If any problems were to arise later, then you will have the chance to settle it legally and will not have to worry about someone or something that might cause issues later.

You should give your lawyer all the right information and ensure that he knows everything there is to about the land and also the properties. He or she will help you draft the division of the land or house amongst all the involved people.

You have to invite everybody that will benefit from it for the hearing in order to make them aware. Once done, every individual will be given their individual papers that they will maintain as their proof for their part of the properties.

Once that is done, they have the right to decide what they wish to do with it. Generally, if there are individual properties then it will be easy for the individuals to dispose them off independently and will not have to worry about what others are doing with their properties. But if it is a single unit that is split many ways then there should be mutual consensus on what needs to be done with the property. A single will not have the right to do anything with it unless everybody else agrees to it.

If no consensus is reached then they will have to settle it based on majority votes.

These are the steps to take in order to settle any inherited property claims in your family, if you are made in charge of it.

Key take aways

Investing in real estate is a good choice for any investor. These investments will help you increase your money's worth over time.

But as you know, it is not easy to invest in real estate properties. The very first thing you must understand is the taxation policy. All governments will levy a certain tax on a property, which the buyer must bear at the time of purchase. The tax will depend on the size of the property. It is important that you remain well versed with the taxation policy in your state.

It is obvious that all people wish to pay lesser taxes and save on some money for themselves. This is quite a bit possible as you can avoid paying taxes by renovating it. There are also other ways in which you can reduce the amount of taxes that you pay on a yearly basis. If you wish to understand it better, then I suggest that you go through the first chapter of this book once again.

When it comes to choosing a property, there are certain things that you need to look into such as the location, size and price of the property. All these are important aspects of any property and it is important that you look into these with a keen eye. Remember that it is extremely important to have an ideal property in mind when you look for your dream property. It is important that you personally inspect the site and look at the different components.

The next choice to make is the type of property to invest in. Whether it is a commercial or a residential or a recreational property, you need to make up your mind on any one of these. Each one comes with its own pros and cons and you must choose the one that fits your needs the best.

Many people choose residential properties to invest in, as they are quite cheap and easily available. People also choose to invest in commercial properties as it is possible to make back your investment money with ease. Recreational properties are also good choices but they come with a lot of responsibility. You can invest in them if you think they are really lucrative and you can make back your money within a set period of time.

The next step is to go about the buying process. You must arrange for the finances, employ a lawyer, contact the owner, draw up a draft etc. All of this will mostly take a week's time.

You must not hurry here and try to remain as patient as possible.

Next, you need to decide what you wish to do with the property. You can move in or rent it out. You can also lease it out if you like. Each of these comes with their individual advantages and disadvantages and so, it is best that you decide on the best one for yourself.

If you are interested in foreign properties then you will have to put in a lot more effort to find the best one. You will also have to bear in mind the different taxation policies and ensure that you are getting a good deal. It is best to take the help of a local expert to find the best property for yourself. The same renting rules apply to your foreign properties.

When you wish to buy a good property, it is important that you consider certain ideal situations. These can include buying in distress sale, buying directly from the owner, buying a property that requires quite a bit of renovation etc. All of these will be available to you for cheap and you can profit from them.

It is best that you look at quick deal options. This is important because property buying generally takes a long time. You need to lessen the time taken to buy and sell in order to get a good deal out of the investment.

It is always a good idea to increase your real estate investments. Don't stick to just one property and mix it up. It is not important that you dispose of your previous property. You can own several properties at once and decide to do different things with it like occupy one, rent out one, lease one etc. You can command a different income from all of these investments.

You can make use of a buy, move and sell strategy. In this type, you buy a property and live there for a couple of years. You then sell it and not pay any taxes on the profit that you earn. This technique is good for all those looking to make a profit from their investment on a regular basis. But there are certain aspects to bear in mind such as not getting too attached to the property, disposing it off at the right time etc.

Container homes are the new rage and they are good investment options for you. You can choose to have a single container home or a couple of them. All you have to do is look for the best land and place a few containers. You can then decorate them in any which way that you like. This type of property is quite an asset and can help you increase your investment options.

When you wish to invest in a property, it is important that you go about it slowly instead of rushing into it. You might end up making a mistake if you go about it too fast. Weigh all your pros and cons before making your decision.

We looked at many countries and their individual pros and cons. You can decide to invest in any one of the countries or multiple ones depending on how much money you have at your disposal. There can be some that will invest in several counties to avail tax benefits and you too can do the same.

Andy Anderson

Conclusion

I thank you once again for choosing this book and hope it succeeded in teaching you a thing or two on the purported topic.

The real estate business is one of the most lucrative fields out there. It offers both individuals and businessmen a good source of earning money and building up an empire of wealth. For the individual, it is an investment that helps him save as much as earn money; buying and selling a property for tax benefits can sound like a daunting task, but once you start doing it, you will understand how simple it is to undertake and execute the operations and how everything can be done in a facile manner.

You must try and be as smart as possible and make all the right moves, in order to have a smooth sailing journey. Remember that you will not be the first one to undertake such operations and will only join the hundreds, who consistently make real estate investments. And once you are familiar with the real estate industry and how it operates, you could branch out into building your real estate business and become a real estate agent.

Once you start breaking into profits, you can begin to set up a wealthy empire and further invest your money to help it grow in value. I wish you all the luck with your real estate ventures and hope you get to save big on your property tax and put the money to good use.

If you received value from this book, then I would like to ask you for a favor. Would you be kind enough to leave a review for this book on Amazon?

Thank you so much!

Check out my other books

Below you'll find some of my other popular books that are popular on Amazon and Kindle as well. Alternatively, you can visit my author page on Amazon to see other work done by me.

Affiliate Marketing: How to make money and create an income in Online Marketing & Internet Marketing

Online Business: Financial Freedom by Building a Successful Online Empire - Home Business, Online Marketing, Business Plan, and Leadership

Small Business: Blueprint on How to start and build a successful Business from Scratch - Startup, Entrepreneur, and Business Ideas

Andy Anderson